Memory and Topography
Orhan Pamuk and the Urban Space

Memory and Topography
Orhan Pamuk and the Urban Space

Dr. Pratyush Ranjan Padhee
Meghna Gupta

BLACK EAGLE BOOKS
Dublin, USA | Bhubaneswar, India

Black Eagle Books
USA address:
7464 Wisdom Lane
Dublin, OH 43016

India address:
E/312, Trident Galaxy, Kalinga Nagar,
Bhubaneswar-751003, Odisha, India

E-mail: info@blackeaglebooks.org
Website: www.blackeaglebooks.org

First International Edition Published by
Black Eagle Books, 2025

MEMORY AND TOPOGRAPHY
ORHAN PAMUK AND THE URBAN SPACE
by **Dr. Pratyush Ranjan Padhee | Meghna Gupta**

Copyright © Dr. Pratyush Ranjan Padhee | Meghna Gupta

All rights reserved. No part of this publication may be reproduced, stored in a retrieval system, or transmitted, in any form or by any means, electronic, mechanical, photocopying, recording or otherwise without the prior permission of the publisher.

Cover & Interior Design: Ezy's Publication

ISBN- 978-1-64560-799-1 (Paperback)

Printed in the United States of America

"I sometimes think that what binds me to the city is not what I remember, but what I have forgotten"

— Orhan Pamuk

CONTENTS

Chapter-1
Introduction-
Orhan Pamuk, Memory and Space   19

Chapter-2
The Texturality of Istanbul-
History, Memory, and Topoimagination   43

Chapter-3
Restoring Memory through Urban Planning   75

Chapter-4
The Spatialization of Trauma:
Sites of Violence and Forgetting
in a Global Context   140

Chapter-5
Conclusion-Towards a Memory-Based
Urban Consciousness   170

Preface

Memory constructs a city as much as bricks and mortar do. It lingers in streets, façades, and silences, shaping the way we perceive and belong to space. This book explores the subtle interplay between memory, topography, and urban planning, tracing how personal recollections disturb and reinterpret official narratives of the city. Grounded in Orhan Pamuk's *Istanbul: Memories and the City* and guided by Henri Lefebvre's notion of conceived space, it examines how memory unsettles the homogenizing impulse of the modern urban imagination. Extending beyond literary analysis, this book engages with urban practice and planning. It argues for **memory-sensitive urbanism,** an approach where planning and architecture operate as acts of remembrance rather than instruments of erasure. These hegemonic narratives, shaped by state mechanisms of power, nationalist aesthetics, and urban planning discourses, often seek to produce a sanitized, linear, and homogenized spatial imaginary. Through a methodological synthesis of textual analysis and spatial hermeneutics, the study argues that Pamuk's narrative in particular and urban planning in general transcend mere cartographic representation of the city. Rather, it evokes a profoundly affective and memory-saturated geography, constructing an alternative topography that foregrounds fragmentation, palimpsestic layering, and emotional resonance. In Pamuk's rendering, Istanbul emerges not as a static locus but as a dynamic, re-inscribed space, a palimpsest of overlapping memories, emotions, and histories that actively disrupt monolithic state-sponsored urban imaginaries.

This book extends beyond literary and theoretical inquiry into a pragmatic, transdisciplinary realm where cultural memory converges with the ethics of spatial restoration. It reimagines urban planning as an act of remembrance rather than erasure, proposing a framework for *memory-sensitive urbanism* that treats the past as an active agent in contemporary design. Central to this vision is the integration of Heritage Impact Assessments (HIA) and participatory planning models that engage both tangible and intangible heritage community narratives, affective geographies, and emotional cartographies that shape urban identity.

Bridging theory and practice, the book engages with exemplary urban designs, including the adaptive renewal of Dadabhai Naoroji Road in Mumbai, the restoration of the Birkha Bawari Stepwell in Jodhpur, and Seoul's Seoullo 7017 project to illustrate how memory-informed design reshapes the experience of the modern city. Each case exemplifies how memory-led design transforms preservation into continuity: Naoroji Road reconciles colonial aesthetics with modern infrastructure; Birkha Bawari revives vernacular hydrological wisdom through sustainable reinterpretation; and Seoullo 7017 converts an obsolete overpass into a living urban archive, fusing history with modernity. Through such examples, the book advances the argument that memory preservation is not aesthetic nostalgia but a form of spatial justice. It calls for architecture to transcend material form and embrace an *ethics of remembrance*, a design philosophy attuned to layered histories and collective memory. Bridging theoretical reflection and urban praxis, this work envisions restoration as a dialogic process balancing modern exigencies with mnemonic depth. Ultimately, it invites planners, conservationists, and scholars to view the city as a living archive where architecture, history, and memory coexist dynamically, and where design becomes a moral act of remembering.

By centering the emotional geography that permeates Pamuk's writing, the book elucidates memory as an active, performative force in the construction and continual transformation of urban meaning. The inquiry is structured around three critical questions such as, How does state-controlled urban planning intersect or collide with Pamuk's subjective remapping of Istanbul? In what ways does personal memory become a critical tool of urban reconstruction? And the central rationale of this book lies in guiding future urban planners to envision cities where development does not come at the cost of erasing historical memory. It urges planners to integrate the past into the spatial logic of the present, designing with sensitivity to inherited structures, cultural landscapes, and lived histories. Such an approach ensures that modernization becomes a process of continuity rather than rupture, allowing urban growth to coexist with the enduring memory of place. By addressing these questions, this book seeks to reveal the profound reciprocity between memory and urban space, positioning the city not as a fixed artifact but as a living text negotiated between personal and collective histories. The implications extend beyond literary criticism into the realm of urban and town planning. It advocates for an urban planning attentive to the mnemonic and affective layers embedded in built environments, one that recognizes preservation not as nostalgia but as a form of cultural continuity. In this fashion, this study envisions a future where development(urban planning) and memory coexist, where architecture and planning sustain the emotional and historical topography of the city rather than effacing it.

Acknowledgement

Dr. Pratyush Ranjan Padhee

It all began on a very hectic day at the University, when Meghna approached me with her keen interest in Orhan Pamuk and the entanglements of memory. Her enthusiasm stirred in me a deep sense of recognition, for memory has always been the axis of my own scholarly pursuit. Encouraging her to pursue this discourse of inquiry was not merely an act of mentorship; it was a reaffirmation of my own intellectual journey ever since my doctorate days, one that has long circled how spaces remember, how cities speak, and how literature restores what time erases.

This book emerged through many such conversations between memory and topography, between the personal and the political, between the silences of trauma and the eloquence of the city. I owe profound gratitude to Meghna who has contributed to the shaping of this work through her questions, challenges, and insights. What began as a daunting and laborious pursuit after long hours of professional commitment, sustained through countless late nights of revision and reflection, has finally seen the light of day. The journey, though demanding, has been deeply fulfilling, transforming perseverance into creation and an everlasting memory.

My heartfelt thanks to the stellar researchers in the field of Memory studies i.e. Andreas Huyssen, Pierre Nora, James E. Young, and Dr. Avishek Parui, whose writings have not only guided and encouraged us to actualise this idea into a book but also continue to inspire contemporary discourse in Memory studies. I am also deeply indebted to the Indian Network for Memory Studies at IIT Madras for providing a space where intellectual memory finds new resonances and dialogues.

To my family and loved ones, thank you for grounding me when my thoughts were adrift among archives, urban ruins, and of course the relentless drafting of the same. On a special note, I extend my deepest gratitude to my close friend, Ms. Purnita Bhatnagar, whose reflections have quietly shaped this book. During our unhurried conversations over coffee, she would often muse that "humans are often frightened by good memories, while sometimes it is the painful ones that bring a strange peace." Those subjective words of hers lingered, finding their way into the heart of this work. As a matter of fact, kudos to Meghna, whose initial spark rekindled the journey of this book, a journey that, in many ways, began with her simple yet profound question: "Why do we remember?"

Acknowledgement

Meghna Gupta

This research has been more than just an academic pursuit; it has been a personal journey of reflection, resilience, and rediscovery. Through every chapter, I have come to understand that architecture is not just about space or structure but about the human capacity to remember, rebuild, and reimagine. My work, much like the cities it studies, is shaped by memory and persistence, the quiet determination to create meaning out of complexity. I, Meghna, owe my deepest gratitude to my parents; their patience and support which have grounded me through uncertainty and inspired me to move forward with purpose. From them, I have learned that ambition is not about reaching higher goals alone but about holding on to humility while striving to create something lasting. They have been my first teachers in endurance, the living proof that roots make growth possible. My heartfelt appreciation goes to my Guide/Mentor, Dr. Pratyush Ranjan Padhee, Sir for his invaluable guidance and belief in my potential. His thoughtful mentorship gave direction to my ideas and shaped them with intellectual precision and emotional depth.

Under his supervision, I discovered that research is not just about gathering information but about listening to spaces, to silences, and to the histories that breathe within both. His trust allowed me to think freely yet responsibly, helping me find my own voice as a scholar. Without him, this book would not have been finished. I am also deeply grateful to the scholars and thinkers whose insights have guided my writing and thought. The works of Henri Lefebvre, Sibel Bozdoğan, and Aleida Assmann and Dr. Avishek Parui among others, provided the theoretical foundation for this exploration of space, memory, and urban identity. Their ideas became the scaffolding on which this work stands. As Dr. Avishek Parui writes, "Memory is not merely the act of looking back; it is the continuity of being, the endurance of emotion across time." These words mirror the essence of this study, reminding me that every place, whether scarred by trauma or sanctified by devotion, holds within it the endurance of the human spirit. To my fellow researchers and friends, I extend my thanks for their encouragement and honest conversations. Their companionship has offered unwavering intellectual and emotional support through the extended hours of reading, revising, and inquiry.

Finally, to the cities that have inspired and shaped my imagination, Amritsar, Delhi, Bhubaneswar, Puri, and Istanbul, thank you for teaching me how architecture can be a form of storytelling, even if I have not walked your streets in person but only through the narratives that bring you alive.

Each city has shown me how memory dwells in walls, in courtyards, in ruins, and in renewal. This work carries a part of my ambition, to contribute meaningfully to the study of space, memory, and identity, and a quiet pride in knowing that persistence and reflection can turn uncertainty into creation. Hence, I stand here not as an author alone but as a student of time, space, and memory, with a spirit of learning and building.

"Forgetting is the best way to remember."
- Aminatta Forna

Chapter – 1

Introduction

Orhan Pamuk, Memory and Space

In the intricate narrative universe of the Turkish Nobel Laureate Orhan Pamuk, memory and space do not merely serve as passive backdrops but function as active agents of identity formation, historical reckoning, and political commentary. Pamuk's literary imagination, deeply embedded in the urban topography of Istanbul, reflects the city's contested histories, layered memories, and the ambivalent relationship between modernity and tradition. His works engage with the palimpsestic character of urban space, where personal and collective memories interweave with the architectural and cultural fabric of the city, exposing the tensions of forgetting and remembering in post-Ottoman Turkey. This chapter investigates the interconnection between memory and space, specifically in the context of Orhan Pamuk's memoir, *Istanbul-Memories and the city.*

Scholars such as Pierre Nora have argued that "sites of memory" (lieux de mémoire) emerge precisely where the organic transmission of memory is threatened by historical discontinuity, thereby becoming deliberate constructs that mediate between past and present (Nora 7). Pamuk's

Istanbul exemplifies such lieux de mémoire, where mosques, museums, old neighbourhoods, and decaying mansions function as mnemonic landscapes that embody historical amnesia and resistance. Similarly, Henri Lefebvre's concept of the social production of space emphasizes that space is not a neutral container but is produced and reproduced through social practices, power relations, and memory work. (Lefebvre 26) Pamuk's narrative techniques, his meticulous descriptions of urban detail, the interplay of fiction and historiography, and the layering of narrative time underscore how space becomes a contested site for remembering, forgetting, and re-imagining identity.

Moreover, the psychoanalytic dimension of memory and space is central to Pamuk's literary works. Maurice Halbwachs's foundational insight that memory is socially framed and spatially situated (Halbwachs 45), parallels well with Pamuk's portrayal of characters in their personal recollections which is inextricably linked to the socio-political architecture of Istanbul. These individual memories interact with collective national narratives, challenging monolithic historical discourses and offering a subaltern counter-memory that complicates official historiography. Theorists like Aleida and Jan Assmann from the discourse of memory studies further highlight the tension between communicative memory (rooted in everyday experience and oral transmission) and cultural memory (institutionalized and codified across generations) (Assmann and Czaplicka 126). Pamuk's work articulates this interplay through his narrative strategies that juxtapose intimate recollections with archival histories, mythic pasts with fragmented urban present.

"Space is never empty. It is always inhabited by memory, power, and ideology" (Lefebvre 26). Space is not merely a geographical entity but a spatio-mnemonic construct. This insight by Henri Lefebvre encapsulates the central concern of this chapter, which explores the intricate interplay between memory and space in the discussed novel of Orhan Pamuk. In Pamuk's literary world, the city of Istanbul emerges not merely as a geographical backdrop but as a palimpsest where personal recollections, collective histories, and political narratives coexist in a constant state of tension. The urban topography of Istanbul becomes a living archive of memory, marked by layers of imperial grandeur, nationalistic rupture, and individual trauma. Pamuk's work demonstrates how space, far from being a neutral or passive entity, is actively produced and reproduced through cultural practices of remembering and forgetting, echoing Lefebvre's argument about the social production of space. Through his detailed descriptions of decaying mansions, historical landmarks, and shifting neighborhoods, Pamuk reveals how spaces are inscribed with ideologies, contested memories, and forgotten histories, thus complicating/challenging the dominant narratives of identity, modernity, and nationhood.

By drawing upon key theoretical frameworks in memory and space studies, including the works of Pierre Nora, Lefebvre, Halbwachs, and the Assmanns, this study situates Pamuk's oeuvre within discourse of memory, space, and urban topography. Pamuk's Istanbul emerges as a palimpsest where memory and space coexist in a constant state of tension, producing a narrative terrain that is at once haunted, contested, and hopeful.

The connection between stories and architecture in literature mirrors the city's buildings, and how architecture, in turn, influences stories, shaping Istanbul's unique character. Memories impact our emotions. A very crucial phrase *Huzun* has been frequently mentioned in Pamuk's novel, which translates to an overbearing feeling of melancholy. Moreover, it also explores nostalgia as a powerful emotion that links people to their past. Moving through history, it clarifies the city's transformation from the Ottoman era to today's Turkish Republic, showing how these changes influence collective memories and identities. Growing up in Istanbul gives Pamuk's account a heartfelt, genuine touch. Moreover, his reflections on childhood, family, and society create a portrait that is both personal and public. He ties these experiences to the city's physical spaces, which help shape his sense of who he is in the present and influence his writing. Landmarks like Hagia Sophia stand out as symbols of Istanbul's layered history, representing the ongoing dialogue between the city's past and present. It's beyond a memoir; it's a thoughtful exploration of how places shape us and how our memories shape the city, making a meaningful contribution to both literature and cultural studies.

Intersection of East/West-

The Literary Oeuvre of Orhan Pamuk is repleted with the profound tension that arises from the interplay between his Eastern lineage and his exposure to Western influences. Raised within the confines of a Westernised, upper-middle-class Turkish household, yet concurrently immersed in the dwindling vestiges of the once-mighty Ottoman Empire, Pamuk's personal and literary experiences exemplify the cultural dichotomy that pervades contemporary Turkey. This dichotomy is not merely a thematic element within his narratives; rather, it is an intrinsic aspect of his existential framework.

A closer inspection elucidates the extent to which European representations of the city have moulded his perceptual apparatus. To Pamuk; "I had grown up with the Western image of Istanbul and saw my city through their eyes" (Pamuk 56). This statement not only serves to critique the Orientalist gaze but also underscores the psychological process of internalisation that such representations engender. This phenomenon, in turn, distorts and reconfigures individual and collective identities. Through his literary endeavours, Pamuk acts as a cultural interlocutor, bridging the aesthetic and ideological chasm that separates the East from the West, yet never succumbing to the false allure of synthesis.

While aligning himself with secularist principles, Pamuk imbues his characters with a complexity that transcends the religious-secular binary. Their lives are suffused with Islamic values that inform their emotional and ethical paradigms, thereby challenging the notion of a monolithic secular existence. In this manner, he critiques the rigidity of ideological dogmas on both sides of the divide, advocating instead for a more inclusive and nuanced understanding of national identity.

Istanbul as a Narrative Space of Convergence, Pamuk's portrayal of Istanbul extends beyond the realm of a mere setting; it assumes the role of a protagonist. The city is depicted as a repository of historical narratives, layered with the detritus of past civilisations, memories, and architectural relics. His reflection on the city's impact on his own identity is encapsulated in the following statement:

"Istanbul's ruins made me who I am" (Pamuk 24). This assertion underscores the symbiotic relationship between personal biography and the geographical landscape. Drawing upon the theoretical framework espoused by Lefebvre, who posits that space is not merely perceived but experienced, Pamuk constructs an Istanbul that is palpable, shape-shifting, and profoundly intertwined with the historical, cultural, and political transformations of his country. For Pamuk, memory functions as the linchpin that ties individual narratives to the broader fabric of collective history. He vehemently resists the tendency to erase Ottoman heritage in the quest for a Westernised national identity. In *The Museum of Innocence,* he constructs a tangible edifice of memory, a museum brimming with artefacts of lost love and forgotten eras. Similarly, *Istanbul: Memories and the City* serve as an autobiographical treatise on visual culture, wherein antiquated photographs, dilapidated structures, and familial silences are imbued with historical significance.

Growing up and living in Istanbul influences his stories, as he mixes the city's rich history with personal experiences. His books focus on what makes Istanbul special, its mix of different cultures, old traditions, and modern changes. Novels like *My Name is Red* and *Snow* bring to life the streets, famous sites, and diverse people of Istanbul, showing the struggle between keeping traditions intact while welcoming the new. In *The Museum of Innocence,* he looks at how memories can hold us back or keep us connected to the past. His characters' stories make us think about how memories affect who we are and how we see the world.

Cultural conflicts are also a key part of his stories. Pamuk often explores tensions in Turkish society, like the fight between secular and religious ideas, old traditions versus new ways, and East versus West. His characters' interactions make us think about societal biases and cultural differences. What makes Pamuk's style phenomenal is how he combines public history with personal stories, drawing from his deep connection to Istanbul. This kind of amalgamation makes his stories feel real and meaningful, helping readers everywhere reflect on what it means to be human, understand themselves better, and deal with society's complexities. His writing has had a big influence on modern literature, especially in how it explores Turkish identity. Through vivid and evocative language, Pamuk encourages readers to question their beliefs, develop empathy, and better understand cultural and personal struggles. Overall, Pamuk's work emphasises the importance of memory, cultural conversations, and individual identity. He's a key voice in literature today. His stories continue to make us think about human nature and changes in society, leaving a strong mark on the literary world.

Orhan Pamuk's Istanbul offers a heartfelt and poetic look at the city, combining personal stories with detailed historical and cultural insights. Pamuk shares his memories of growing up in Istanbul alongside its complex and layered history, providing a close and personal view of a city balancing East and West, tradition and modern life. With vivid language and a deep affection for his hometown, Pamuk draws readers into the soul of Istanbul, displaying its beauty, struggles, and lasting magnetism. Pamuk rediscovers his identity in *Istanbul: Memories and the city* as he mentions ; "Istanbul's fate is my fate: I am attached to this city because it has made me who I am" (Pamuk 26).

In this blending of personal and historical city the first chapter of the novel titled 'Another Orhan' recalls his childhood from a very young age as he says;

"I suspected there was more to my world than I could see, somewhere in the streets of Istanbul, in a house resembling ours, there lived another Orhan so much like me that he could pass for my twin, even my double. I can't remember where I got this idea or how it came to me. It must have emerged from a web of rumours, misunderstanding, illusions and fears. But in one of my earliest memories, it is already clear how I've come to feel about my ghostly other". (Pamuk 12).

Orhan Pamuk's Istanbul: Memories and the City blends autobiography with the city's layout and collective memory. It shows how Istanbul's physical spaces and imagination shape identity, mixing personal stories with cultural insights. It discusses how their grandparents' business prospered during the early days of the Turkish Republic which also examines how the family adapted to life in Istanbul and emphasises the lively atmosphere of a Turkish household. The home is decorated with numerous items that seem more suited for display rather than everyday use, emphasising the tension between modernity and tradition. Orhan reflects on the importance of appearances in their culture and describes a photo of his grandparents, providing insight into their traditional and cultural values. Pamuk's childhood home in Nişantaşı, a district on Istanbul's European side, serves as a microcosm of the city's social and architectural transitions. The family apartment building, described as a "museum" of republican-era reflects the tension between Ottoman heritage and modernist reforms. Pamuk walks through neighbourhoods like Beyoğlu(a municipality district in Istanbul) and along the shores of the Bosphorus show how his relationship with Istanbul is changing. He's exploring the city's unique blend of old and new, where crumbling Ottoman mansions sit beside shiny high-rises and Byzantine ruins beside modern concrete buildings. These walks feel like a way for him to 'read' the city's complicated, broken-up identity. Moreover, he shares his thoughts on this as he wanders, creating a vivid tapestry of these fascinating personal recollections and reflections, as the memoir delves into the author's psyche. Living in Istanbul means being surrounded by a city full of stories from the past. The author's home reflects this deep history through artefacts and cultural traces that whisper tales of days gone by. There's a photograph of the author's grandfather standing next to a car, an image that whispers of success and hints at something even greater, the rich cultural and historical mixture of this place. This photo offers a peek into a time long before ours, woven tightly with the legacy of the Ottoman Empire. For over 600 years, the empire was a bright, diverse civilisation celebrated for its stunning architecture, bright arts, and rich trade. You can still see its influence today in the region's beautiful buildings, colourful markets, and cultural traditions. The narrator feels a warm sense of pride and a deep connection to this heritage, seeing their grandparents as living symbols of a long-standing legacy that helps shape their identity. Even though the empire has long since fallen, its spirit continues to live on through modern culture, sparking appreciation for history, resilience, and cherished traditions. Remembering and honouring these parts of the past feels more important than ever in our changing world. That photograph stands as a powerful reminder of the sacrifices and strength handed down through generations. As to Dr. Parui photographs serve as markers for facilitating the interaction between digital and physical spaces to reconstruct and experience collective memories. (Parui12) It emphasises how major cultural legacy and personal history are structured showing how the Ottoman Empire's legacy still influences regional identity and culture today.

Living in Istanbul feels like being surrounded by history every day. My apartment is full of artefacts and photos that tell stories about my heritage. One photo of my grandfather with a new car sticks with me; it's a symbol of success and reflects the cultural values tied to the Ottoman Empire's legacy. The Ottoman Empire, once a powerful and diverse civilisation, played a huge role in shaping culture, science, arts, architecture, and global trade across the regions it covered. Even today, you can still see its influence in the architecture, markets, art, and traditions, which all remind us of a resilient and rich historical legacy. The narrator mentions,

" Looking at that photo makes me feel proud and deeply connected to where I come from. It's a piece of history that has been passed down through generations, shaping who I am today and what I value. Remembering my roots helps me appreciate the cultural richness, the triumphs, and even the struggles that continue to influence us now. The Ottoman legacy inspires me with a sense of strength and resilience, showing how important it is to honour our history while welcoming change and growth." (Pamuk 79)

Urban space is an intricate tapestry of interwoven forces, where the fabric of the environment is not merely a passive stage but rather an active participant in the unfolding of human experience. This dynamic is particularly evident in the case of Istanbul, a city situated at the nexus of continents and histories, where individual and collective identities coalesce and diverge. The theoretical underpinning of this book is derived from Henri Lefebvre's seminal concept of "conceived space," which posits that the configuration of urban environments is not exclusively physical but is also profoundly influenced by abstract ideas and the exercise of power (Lefebvre 38). Lefebvre's triadic model, comprising spatial practice, representations of spaces, provides an essential analytical tool for dissecting the multidimensionality of cities. This framework is instrumental in comprehending how urban landscapes are not solely the product of structured planning and governance but are equally shaped by the lived experiences and remembered pasts of their inhabitants.

Pamuk's memoir serves as a compelling example of the ways in which personal recollection can both challenge and enrich prevailing notions of urban space and topography. His narrative does not merely offer a nostalgic glance at the city of his youth rather constitutes a form of spatial intervention that counters the sanitized and often reductive representations commonly found in institutional and official discourses. This intervention is aligned with the perspective of geographer Doreen Massey, who maintains that space is inherently dynamic and constructed through an intricate web of global and local interrelations (Massey 9). Massey's assertion underscores the significance of personal memory as an agent of spatial transformation, contributing to the continuous reconfiguration of the city's identity.

The memoir transcends the confines of traditional autobiography by acting as a counter-narrative that resists the erasure of historical depth and cultural complexity that often accompany processes of modernization. As theorized by scholars such as Andreas Huyssen, memory can function as a potent tool of "counter-memory," destabilizing dominant historical discourses and opening avenues for marginalized perspectives (Huyssen 7). Through the evocation of melancholy *(hüzün)* and nostalgia, Pamuk imbues the city with an emotional topography that is frequently omitted from formal cartographic representations, thereby asserting the presence of subjective experience in the urban fabric.

The memoir confronts and deconstructs institutionalised spatial imaginaries, thereby exposing the underlying tensions between the imagined and the experienced city. It deconstructs institutionalized spatial imaginaries, exposing the tension between the imagined and the experienced city. Drawing on Pierre Nora's concept of *lieux de mémoire*, Pamuk's memoir positions Istanbul itself as a living site of memory, where official narratives and personal recollections coexist in an unstable dialogue. As Nora (1989) suggests, memory sites emerge when spontaneous memory fades, becoming institutionalized and objectified through monuments, museums, and state-sponsored narratives. However, Pamuk resists this institutionalization by presenting the city as layered and ambiguous, a palimpsest where multiple temporalities intersect. This resonates with Dr. Avishek Parui's insight that memory is spatially and digitally mediated. Similarly,

Gaston Bachelard (1994) argues in *The Poetics of Space* that space is not merely physical but profoundly imaginative, shaped by personal experience and memory. Pamuk illustrates this by recounting how childhood experiences in Istanbul are inextricably linked to specific streets and buildings, stating, "Istanbul is a city where one walks a tightrope between history and the present, where every street is haunted by the ghosts of conflicting pasts." (Pamuk 58) Furthermore, Michel Foucault's theory of heterotopias illuminates Pamuk's spatial exploration of memory, as the city functions as a heterotopic space where multiple, often contradictory, narratives coexist. The memoir thus becomes an act of resistance against the homogenizing tendencies of official historiography, foregrounding how memory is enacted through space rather than merely represented. In doing so, Pamuk's narrative exemplifies the performative and contested nature of memory, showing that space is never empty but always inscribed by power, ideology, and personal recollection (Parui and Raj, 2023).

Memory, Space and the City

Memory plays a fundamental role in how individuals and communities experience and understand urban space. The city is not simply a physical construct of streets, buildings, and infrastructure; it is also a dynamic, affective landscape shaped by personal and collective recollections. Memories inscribe the city with layers of meaning, transforming its material presence into a living palimpsest where past and present coexist. In this context, space becomes more than a neutral backdrop. It emerges as an active site of memory production, contestation, and resistance. Henri Lefebvre's concept of "conceived space" emphasizes how institutional powers and state-driven urban planning impose official spatial narratives, yet subjective memory disrupts these frameworks by revealing hidden histories, emotions, and experiences that resist standardization. Thus, memory and urban space are deeply intertwined, as acts of remembering reconfigure the city from a static entity into a mutable memoryscape, rich with personal stories, silenced voices, and affective geographies. This interplay invites a critical rethinking of the city as not merely constructed by politics and ideology, but continuously rewritten through the flux of remembering and forgetting.

The core issues of this book lie in the discussion of Istanbul's urban identity, focusing on how memory, architecture, and space reconstruct the identity of the subject in the city. Personal and shared memories influence Istanbul's character amidst its history and how architecture and literature affect perceptions of identity, and reflect collective memory. The endeavour in this book considers Istanbul's developing cultural identity amidst swift growth and globalisation, drawing critical insights from sociology, architecture, and literature. Politics and history influence personal and public narratives and investigate everyday social and cultural practices that reinforce the city's unique identity. Hence it is important to note that, it's about understanding what makes Istanbul special/spatially unique and how its history and memories shape its present in the context of memory, space, and topography.

Memory, particularly as articulated through literary narratives, contests and reshapes official spatial imaginaries. Central to this inquiry is an exploration of how collective and individual memories influence Istanbul's urban identity; how architecture both sustains and transforms mnemonic traces over time; and how narrative, as a cultural practice, reflects the everyday experiences of the city's inhabitants. The study adopts an interdisciplinary framework, drawing on insights from urban studies, memory studies, architecture, literary criticism, and cultural theory to critically interrogate established representations of the city. It places particular emphasis on cultural dynamics, lived experience, and community memory, aiming to challenge reductive or homogenized understandings of Istanbul's spatial identity. The city of Istanbul is not merely a passive backdrop in this work but is instead posited as a significant character with an active role in shaping the narrative. The text embodies a series of vignettes, interspersed with photographic elements, that together contribute to a nuanced comprehension of the city as a multidimensional construct. The interplay of personal and communal recollections within the framework of the city's physical and emotional landscape underscores the significance of memory in defining urban identity. A prevalent motif as discussed earlier within "Istanbul: Memories and the City" is the concept of "hüzün," which is frequently translated as "melancholy." However, in the context of Pamuk's narrative, *hüzün* encompasses a collective feeling of loss, longing, and nostalgia. This emotional disposition is omnipresent in the author's reminiscences and functions as a conceptual lens through which the city's infrastructure, historical remnants, and quotidian activities are examined. Gönül Pultar astutely observes that "Pamuk's Istanbul is a city haunted by its imperial past, its dwindling splendour, and its persistent yearning for what once was" (Pultar113).

The notion of *hüzün* transcends individual sentiment and emerges as a shared urban phenomenon that unites the city's populace within a collective memory. The cityscape, characterized by dilapidated mansions along the Bosphorus, atmospheric streets shrouded in fog, and vestiges of Ottoman grandeur, exemplifies a layered historical presence a palimpsest of recollections that stands in opposition to the monolithic narratives of progress and renewal promoted by official histories. In this capacity, Pamuk's memoir can be regarded as a form of intellectual resistance against the eradication of collective memory by state-driven accounts of urban planning advancement.

Azade Seyhan has eloquently highlighted how "Pamuk's memoir deconstructs the monolithic image of Istanbul promoted by nationalist discourse, providing instead a fragmented, polyphonic vision that underscores the city's multifaceted nature and complexity" (Seyhan 178). The author's meticulous portrayals of neighbourhoods, thoroughfares, and private spaces redefine the city through the emotional and personal connotations they evoke, thereby challenging the reductive nature of official cartographies. The inclusion of photographs, both historical and familial, serves as a distinctive feature of the memoir. These visual elements operate as post memory, a term introduced by Marianne Hirsch, which bridges personal recollections with the broader historical tapestry. (Hirsch, 22) The juxtaposition of images from different eras constructs a visual archive that problematizes the linear progression of historical narratives

Pamuk's engagement with photography also encapsulates his ambivalence towards the city's transformation. As Pelin Kıvrak suggests, "The photographs in the memoir are not mere illustrations; they are memory-sites, fragments of a vanished world that persist in the present" (Kıvrak 95). The act of viewing these images is thus imbued with a sense of wailing, serving to preserve the traces of a city that is perpetually evolving.

A collective sense of melancholy and loss is deeply embedded within the city's identity. His vivid portrayal of Istanbul diverges from the stereotypical representations found in touristic materials or nationalistic narratives. The city emerges as a palimpsest, with each layer of memory and historical event contributing to its complex character. The interconnection between personal and collective memory is paramount in shaping the cityscape, as emphasised by the narrator's assertion that the essence of a city is derived not merely from its tangible edifices but also from the collective aspirations and recollections of its inhabitants. This perspective underscores the significance of subjective memory in constructing urban identity, challenging the Cartesian view of cities as static, rational entities. Pamuk's approach to the city is essentially topographic, yet his mapping is guided by the contours of memory rather than the precision of cartographic lines. The neighbourhoods and landmarks of Istanbul are transformed into storied locales, resonating with the emotional weight of the past. The city's physical degradation, its dilapidated mansions, forgotten industrial areas, and overgrown gardens, metaphorically mirror the attrition of collective memory. However, Pamuk's reflections are devoid of romanticised nostalgia, opting instead for a portrayal suffused with ambivalence and intricacy. The beauty of the city, according to his account, is found not in idealised perfection but in its imperfections, the palpable evidence of its storied past. As he critically notes:

"History becomes a word with no meaning; they take stones from the city walls and add them to the modern materials to make new buildings, or they go about restoring old buildings with concrete" (Pamuk 92).

Through these observations, Pamuk critiques how modernisation can erode historical consciousness. Yet, he also shows how memory persists despite transformation. The physical space of Istanbul acts as a mnemonic device, a bridge between personal and collective experiences. The emotional resonance of the built environment is poignantly captured when he writes:

"Istanbul does not carry its hüzün as an illness for which there is a cure. It carries its hüzün by choice"
(Pamuk 93).

Pamuk also takes a critical stance against official narratives, those that are shaped by government propaganda or Western perceptions, that often portray Istanbul as exotic, picturesque, or romantic. Instead, he invites the reader to see the city's more hidden side: its sense of loss, silence, and the melancholic hüzün that pervades its crumbling architecture and forgotten corners. He observes, "What I saw was not the splendour of empire but the ruins of an inheritance that had become my burden" (Pamuk 46). These words capture how space carries deep historical and emotional weight. Istanbul, in his eyes, becomes a kind of palimpsest, a surface written over many times, where the remnants of empire, personal memories, and contemporary urban plans all coexist and overlap. Through this, Pamuk changes Istanbul into what might be called a memory-scape, an environment shaped by both what we remember and what we have lost. His story encourages readers to see cities not just as collections of buildings and streets, but as living archives teeming with feelings, history, and identity, waiting to be discovered.

Orhan Pamuk's book, *Istanbul: Memories and the City*, is a real gem that shows us how the city's geography is a living storybook. It's like the streets and buildings are telling us tales from centuries ago, with every turn holding a new chapter of history and personal moments. Istanbul isn't just a place; it's like a main character that's been through a lot and has the stories to prove it. Istanbul is full of contrasts. The protagonist's melancholic disposition, therefore, serves not merely as a personal narrative but as a reflection of the city's soul, transforming the memoir into an intricate cartography of emotional topography. As the protagonist observes the transformations within his home and the external cityscape, he experiences a profound sense of displacement. This instability fuels his introspective journey, prompting him to seek solace in the realm of artistic expression, initially through painting, as a means of anchoring himself in a world that seems increasingly transient. The eventual shift from visual art to the written word is portrayed not as a rejection of his past but as a natural progression, a methodological evolution through which he can synthesise the tumultuous interplay of memory, space, and emotion. Writing emerges as a critical act of spatial reclamation, allowing him to inhabit the city anew, reimagining decay as a fertile ground for artistic creation.

Lefebvre's notion of "conceived space," which pertains to the urban environments that are meticulously designed and represented by political and institutional forces. These representations often aim to impose order and coherence, thereby erasing the rich tapestry of personal narratives and diverse experiences. In contrast, Pamuk's counter-narrative constitutes an act of personal reclamation, where his memoirs reconfigure the city's space in a manner that resists institutional sanitisation. The emotional geography of the city is a prominent theme in the work. The author's vivid descriptions of the Bosphorus and the Golden Horn, suffused with melancholic and nostalgic tones, reveal how subjective memory imbues spaces with significance that may not be captured by formal histories or spatial representations . This emotive portrayal underscores the city's role as an active participant in the formation of identity and memory, thereby complicating the notion that urban spaces are merely passive backdrops for human activity. Pamuk's narrative stands as a counterpoint to the official histories of the city, which often seek to impose closure and coherence. To Huyssen by focusing on the persistence of memory, he opens the city's past to multiple interpretations and resistances (Huyssen 12). This act of remembrance becomes a form of opposition to the homogenising forces that have sought to shape Istanbul's identity, whether through the lens of westernisation or modernisation. The architecture of the city is not merely a passive backdrop in this narrative but an active agent in the preservation and transmission of memory. Through meticulous descriptions of Ottoman palaces, traditional wooden houses, and the stark contrast of modernist apartment blocks, Pamuk illustrates how the built environment encapsulates and animates the city's layered history.

Space and Childhood

The narrator's childhood within the confines of a once-magnificent imperial city is now in a state of decay. The narrative is deeply embedded in the phenomenological understanding of space, where the cityscape is not merely an abstract or detached construct but a tangible, visceral reality experienced through the subjective lens of the narrator's youth. The young protagonist's perception of the city is a confluence of architecture and emotion, a lived space shaped by the nuances of his personal experiences rather than by the imposed, rationalistic frameworks of cartography or urban planning. At the outset of the memoir, the narrator expresses a poignant disenchantment that encapsulates the essence of the tension between the conceived space of the city and its lived reality. He recounts:

"I'd been told that Istanbul was the centre of the world, and I believed it. But the centre turned out to be a quiet street in Nişantaşı with nothing very interesting about it" (Pamuk 98).

This inconvenient revelation exemplifies the dichotomy between the conceived space, which represents the idealised representations of a place often constructed by the dominant discursive narratives of history, power, and the lived space, which is a deeply personal and experiential construct suffused with the individual's memories and affective responses. Drawing from Lefebvre's seminal work on the social production of space, one can discern that the narrator's experience is emblematic of how the imposed grandeur of the city is mediated by the personal and the intimate, revealing the complex interplay between the abstract and the concrete, the historical and the individual.

Throughout the narrative, the child's spatial consciousness regarding his childhood is inextricably linked to the intimate domains of the domestic interior and the immediate environs of his neighbourhood. He eloquently articulates; "The black-and-white photographs of our house remind me not of my childhood but of the silence that surrounded it" (Pamuk 36). Here, the silence is not merely an aural phenomenon but an intrinsic component of the space itself, illustrating how the physical structure of the home becomes a conduit for the emotional dynamics that animate the narrator's personal history. In this sense, Lefebvre's theory that space is socially and emotionally produced is vividly brought to life, as the architecture of the house becomes a metaphor for the emotional tensions and introspective moments that characterised the author's formative years. Pamuk's portrayal of the city is suffused with a profound sense of nostalgia, not for the grandeur of the imperial past, but for the mundane yet emotionally resonant scenes of everyday life that imbue the urban fabric with a sense of belonging and loss. As he traverses the streets of Istanbul, he realises; "Every street, every house, every window seemed to harbour secrets" (Pamuk 50). This perspective underscores the idea that the city is not a static backdrop but a living archive of narratives waiting to be discovered, a notion that is reinforced by the concept that the act of walking, observing, and wandering constitutes a form of spatial praxis that allows for the construction of a profound connection to the environment. The ruins of the Ottoman Empire that punctuate the cityscape serve as both historical reminders and deeply personal metaphors for the narrator. Reflecting on these remnants, he states:

"In those crumbling mansions along the Bosphorus, I sensed a sadness that I would one day call hüzün" (Pamuk 79). As mentioned earlier the term *hüzün*, encapsulates a collective sense of melancholy, is not merely an emotional disposition but a spatial atmosphere that the child comes to recognise as an integral part of the city's identity. This observation suggests that the decay and silence of the city are not merely symptomatic of a lived past but are imbued with a profound emotional significance that resonates with the inhabitants on a deeply personal level.

Works Cited
- Assmann, Aleida. *Cultural Memory and Western Civilization: Functions, Media, Archives*. Cambridge University Press, 2011.
- Bachelard, Gaston. *The Poetics of Space*. Translated by Maria Jolas, Beacon Press, 1994.
- Halbwachs, Maurice. *On Collective Memory*. Translated by Lewis A. Coser, University of Chicago Press, 1992.
- Hirsch, Marianne. *The Generation of Postmemory: Writing and Visual Culture After the Holocaust*. Columbia University Press, 2012.
- Huyssen, Andreas. *Present Pasts: Urban Palimpsests and the Politics of Memory*. Stanford University Press, 2003.
- Kıvrak, Pelin. "Urban Imaginaries and the Politics of Memory in Contemporary Istanbul." *Journal of Cultural Memory Studies*, vol. 4, no. 2, 2020, pp. 33–49.
- Lefebvre, Henri. *The Production of Space*. Translated by Donald Nicholson-Smith, Blackwell, 1991.
- Massey, Doreen. *For Space*. Sage Publications, 2005.

- Nora, Pierre. "Between Memory and History: Les Lieux de Mémoire." *Representations*, no. 26, 1989, pp. 7–24.
- Pamuk, Orhan. *Istanbul: Memories and the City*. Translated by Maureen Freely, Knopf, 2005.
- Parui, Avishek. "Memory, Media and the Digital Self." *Memory Studies*, vol. 15, no. 3, 2022, pp. 1–15.
- Pulta, Gonul. "Narrative Memory and Urban Identity in Istanbul." *Memory Studies Review*, vol. 8, no. 1, 2018, pp. 101–118.
- Seyhan, Azade. *Writing Outside the Nation*. Princeton University Press, 2001.

Chapter – 2

The Texturality of Istanbul History, Memory, and Topoimagination

The City as Text: Narratives of Layered Histories

History often begins not with words, but with layers of stone, soil, and memory pressed together like a palimpsest. Istanbul is one of those rare cities where time itself feels alive. Each step along its winding streets uncovers more than a mere trace of the past; it becomes a conversation with ages long buried. Beneath the bustling present, the ground holds fossils, broken ceramics, forgotten foundations, and unrecorded voices, whispering of empires, migrations, and ordinary lives. Cities are not born in a single moment but are written and rewritten, like ancient manuscripts where one text hides beneath another. Istanbul is such a manuscript. To stand at the edge of the Bosphorus is to feel that time itself has folded upon the city, pressing its weight into the stones, the waters, and even the air. Here, the present is never alone. The past breathes beneath it, rising like faint letters that have survived the scrape of the pen.

History in Istanbul does not unfold as a linear narrative; rather, it accumulates in sedimented layers, pressing together human and natural histories into a single palimpsestic surface. The city itself is a dialogue between earth and empire, between stone and imagination, where every street corner and hidden courtyard bears witness to decisions made across centuries. To walk its labyrinthine pathways is not merely to observe but to participate and follow the traces left by emperors and merchants, by anonymous residents, and by the currents of water that once carved this terrain. Memory here is not an inert archive but a living architecture. In this chapter, we propose the term *topoimagination* to describe the imaginative act of engaging with urban topography not only as physical terrain but as a repository of memory, desire, and cultural meaning. Whereas *topography* refers to the material layout of a landscape and *imagination* to the creative processes of meaning-making. Hence, *Topoimagination* captures the fusion of the two: the interpretive and affective practice of "reading" the city as both text and memory-scape. *Topoimagination* renders this process intelligible: it is the hermeneutic practice of reading the city simultaneously as text, map, and echo, discerning how desire, loss, and invention are encoded into its spatial forms.

Beneath the visible Istanbul lie invisible strata of geological and cultural rocks, fossils, buried foundations, and fragments of ceramics which remind us that the city's most ancient narratives are as much geological as they are human. Empires rise and fall, yet the land remembers, preserving the imprint of seas, shifting continents, and climates long vanished. History here is not reducible to dynasties or battles; it is a palpable force circulating through courtyards, staircases, and terraces, binding human ambition to the enduring patience of the earth itself.

Istanbul is thus a city that thinks simultaneously forwards and backwards: its present cannot be conceived apart from the shadows of millennia, nor its imagination apart from memory etched into stone. To traverse its topography is to witness the braiding of natural history, human history, and lived present, each shaping the other and demanding that the observer move from passive gaze to dialogic engagement. The city calls for attention, interpretation, and reflection, offering a model of urban experience in which memory, topoimagination, and history exist as inseparable elements of being.

Here, history is not sequestered in monumental structures but diffuses through courtyards, stairways, and rooftops, always awaiting activation by attentive perception. A doorway, a fading inscription, the angle of a minaret each becomes a point of temporal connection, linking the observer to lives long extinguished. Istanbul's urban fabric operates like a manuscript written across centuries, where the traces of Byzantines, Ottomans, and countless ordinary inhabitants coexist with contemporary interventions. Memory in this context is not static, nor merely nostalgic; it is performative. To walk these streets is to enact remembrance, to negotiate the survival of what endures, and to anticipate the forms through which the future will inscribe itself.

Each layer of Istanbul's topography embodies decision and encounter, a threshold between eras. Graffiti scrawled across Byzantine walls, sunlit terraces suspended above Ottoman courtyards, or modern stairways twisting around ancient stonework each illustrates the ongoing negotiation between continuity and transformation. This is the essence of topoimagination: the recognition that urban space is shaped as much by desire, memory, and imagination as by architecture and planning. The city solicits engagement not as a spectacle but as a participatory text; to traverse its streets is to chart invisible trajectories of time, to sense the resonance of forgotten footsteps, and to allow history itself to converse with the present.

In this way, Istanbul does not simply preserve memory it performs it. Epochs are layered into lived space, enabling past, present, and imagination to coexist. The city thus becomes a canvas of temporal consciousness, demonstrating that inhabiting urban space is always already an act of interpretation, reflection, and creation. For scholars and observers alike, Istanbul exemplifies how history is spatially inscribed and how memory and imagination intersect, offering a model of urban experience at once analytical, immersive, and profoundly human.

Yet to apprehend Istanbul fully, one must move beyond the traces of human presence. Its oldest history is not merely imperial or anthropogenic but profoundly geological. Long before Byzantium, Constantinople, or the modern metropolis, the terrain belonged to seas, drifting continents, and the slow temporality of nature. Fossils of marine life still embedded in its bedrock serve as mute witnesses to epochs when the city was unimaginable yet already in preparation. The soil retains fragments of an age prior to human arrival, preparing the stage for the histories that would later unfold. To imagine Istanbul in this way is to perceive it as a living organism of stone and bone, where natural and human histories share the same skin, each layer informing and shaping the other's memory.

And yet, geology alone does not account for

Istanbul's persistence in cultural imagination. Its resonance is equally anthropological. As Andrew Strathern and Pamela J. Stewart remind us in *Anthropological Perspectives on Landscape, Memory, and History*, "landscapes are never empty canvases; they are living archives of stories, steeped in memory and nourished by belonging" (Strathern & Stewart, p. 45). Istanbul's hills and waters murmur with prayers once lifted beneath Hagia Sophia's dome, thrum with the movement of caravans along the Silk Road, and sigh with the longing of exiles gazing across the Bosphorus.

Here, the land itself becomes a voice: bearing the weight of empires, the rhythms of commerce, the hush of faith, and the ache of dispossession. Spaces endure not simply because they exist but because they are inhabited, remembered, and narrated until the very stones appear to breathe with history. Jan Assmann's theory of *cultural memory* sharpens this insight, showing how societies institutionalize remembrance through monuments, rituals, and collective narratives (Assmann, p. 98). In Istanbul, cultural memory is omnipresent in domes rising like prayers, in Byzantine walls softened by ivy, and in the adhan reverberating across modern highways. Even when stone erodes or inscriptions fade, memory persists, layered like the faint lines of an ancient manuscript.

Paul Ricoeur, in Memory, History, Forgetting, instructs us that memory is never a raw truth. It's formed of forgetting, of imagining, of desiring (Ricoeur 212). Istanbul enshrines this paradox within every stone, every echo. Here rest layers of empire: the majestic domed Hagia Sophia, commissioned by Emperor Justinian between A.D. 532 and 537, filled with its lofty arches and mosaics; the massive Theodosian Walls, built under Theodosius II in A.D. 447, defining the ancient silhouette of the city. Empires collapsed, emperors came and went, but what stays most vibrant within people's hearts are the emotions those monuments bear: loss, longing, triumph, and grief, and the mosaics of the Chora Church from the 14th century, but what lives most strongly in people's hearts are not just the stones but the feelings tied to them: triumph, loss, longing, and sorrow.

Paul Ricoeur observes in *Memory, History, Forgetting* that memory is never raw truth; it is shaped by forgetting, imagining, and desiring (Ricoeur 212). Istanbul enshrines this paradox in every stone and echo. Layers of empire remain: the Hagia Sophia, commissioned by Justinian (A.D. 532–537), with its lofty arches and mosaics; the Theodosian Walls, built under Theodosius II (A.D. 447); and the Chora Church, with its 14th-century mosaics. Beyond human memory, the city preserves nature's deep past: a ten-million-year-old limpet fossil from the Miocene and 145-million-year-old Jurassic fossils within the Republic Monument in Taksim (Hurriyet Daily News, 2015). Memory, both natural and human, coexists in Istanbul's streets, basilicas, and hidden sanctuaries such as Tuzla Değirmenaltı Monastery. Each excavation is a reminder that the past never truly vanishes; it waits quietly beneath the surface, ready to speak again when touched by human hands. For this, in the midst of boulevards, monuments, and modern life, Istanbul still preserves the whispers of ancient seas. The city does not simply rise above history; it drifts upon oceans of memory that flow far beyond the reach of empires. In Istanbul, memory is both real and imagined; it lingers in basilicas transformed into mosques, such as the 6th-century Little Hagia Sophia with its graceful octagonal design, and in the fading frescoes of Chora, painted during Byzantium's final centuries before the Ottoman conquest in A.D. 1453. Yet the memory dwells in silence, in the myths which whisper about the sultans, and in the verses of exiles who once stood on the shore gazing longingly across the Bosphorus. Beneath the modern city, excavations continue to uncover forgotten sanctuaries such as the Tuzla Deirmenalt Monastery, with its church crypt and burial grounds still folded within deeper layers of stone. At each discovery is not only a fragment of the past but also a reminder that the past never truly vanishes; it waits patient and quiet beneath the surface, ready to speak again when touched by human hands.

Unearthings of memory reveals hidden sanctuaries like Tuzla Değirmenaltı Monastery, with its church, crypt, and burial grounds tucked beneath newer layers of the city. It demonstrates that the past is never truly gone; it lingers quietly, waiting to be discovered. Like a palimpsest, Istanbul holds both erased lines and rewritten ones. The layers of natural history remind us of its ancient depths, while the discovery of human remains and monuments reveals its cultural core. From the Bronze Age (c. 3300-1200 B.C.) to the grandeur of Byzantium (A.D. 330-1453), the rise of the Ottomans (A.D. 1453-1922), and the birth of the Republic in A.D. 1923, the city reveals itself layer by layer. Together, these traces remind us that Istanbul is more than just geography. It is a living archive where seashell bones and empires' prayers coexist, each capturing the light of memory in its own unique way.

In Istanbul, the stones themselves seem to remember. Every dome, minaret, and crumbling wall whispers stories of centuries, each one a pearl strung into the city's living necklace. Byzantine arches lean gently beside Ottoman mosques, while modern glass towers rise above streets once traced by imperial processions. Here, old and new do not clash, they converse. The grandeur of past empires does not disappear beneath contemporary life; it lingers in the shadows, the echoes of footsteps on worn cobbles, and the gentle curves of mosaics peeking from hidden corners.

Paleontology compels us to apprehend Istanbul not merely as an assemblage of stone and mortar, but as a corporeal archive of temporality itself. Fossils interred within the substrata function as voices from deep antiquity, narrating histories of receding seas, vanished climates, and life forms antecedent to the empires that would later line the Bosphorus. To encounter these stratifications is to apprehend the deliberate cadence of nature pressing upon the ephemeral gestures of human existence, to perceive a memory of the city extending far beyond the bounds of nominative comprehension. For the residents of istanbul, such echoes evoke both awe and melancholy: an acute awareness that the streets and domiciles upon which their tread are suspended atop a temporality far more expansive than the immediacy of their lives, and that certain once-vibrant presences endure only as quiet shadows impressed into stone.

Yet Istanbul's memory is not reducible to geological inscription alone. The city's landscapes are suffused with human narratives interwoven with natural transformation, as Strathern and Stewart underscore in *Anthropological*

Perspectives on Landscape, Memory, and History (Strathern and Stewart 45). Each ruin, alleyway, and monument resonates with traces of antecedent actors. The Hagia Sophia, for instance, exists not merely as an architectural artifact; it pulsates with centuries of devotional practice, triumph, and grief. Even the ostensibly forgotten walls murmur, linking past existences with the contemporary rhythm of urban life. Among Istanbulites, this produces a nuanced melancholia: an acknowledgment that neighborhoods evolve, traditions dissipate, yet quotidian life persists. Some alterations are experienced as burdens; others are absorbed as tacit acquiescence to the city's inexorable temporal flow Memory in Istanbul is simultaneously ephemeral and enduring. As Jan Assmann elucidates, cultural memory transcends a mere repository of factual knowledge; it constitutes a dynamic system through which personal experiences are transmuted into collective narratives and symbolic forms, sustaining communal dialogue with the past (*Cultural Memory and Early Civilization*, 24). Forgetting, therefore, does not signify obliteration; it constitutes an additional stratum within the palimpsestic cityscape, a new surface inscribed over antecedent narratives (Assmann 28). This process of layering is palpably manifested throughout Istanbul for example in the faded Byzantine mosaics, the weathered Ottoman inscriptions, and even in the graffiti etched upon stone walls. Such inscriptions do not efface prior histories; rather, they integrate them into emergent stories, so that each ruin, shadow, and marking functions simultaneously as a testament to both remembering and forgetting.

Paul Ricoeur reminds us that memory is never fixed; it is always shaped by imagination and choice (*Memory,*

History, Forgetting 23). Istanbul makes this visible. Here, human memory is intertwined with geological memory: fossils in the stone walls, shells along the Bosphorus, bones in the soil. Time in the city is layered, natural time and human history weave together like threads in a single fabric. For the residents of Istanbul, this is not only abstract; it is something they live. They see themselves as heirs of beauty and sorrow, carrying forward memories that are both gift which they cherish and a burden which they can never retrieve in physical form.

As Pierre Nora writes, certain places become *lieux de mémoire*, "sites of memory", where history and feeling crystallize and resist being forgotten (Nora 27). In Istanbul, every mosque, square, and bazaar serves as such a site, charged with memory. This matches Henri Lefebvre's insight that space is not an empty background but lived, shaped, and remembered through daily practice.

Orhan Pamuk deepens this idea in his novel *Istanbul: Memories and the City* through the concept of **hüzün**, a collective melancholy that belongs to the city itself. (Discussed in Chapter 1) He writes:

"If I am to convey the intensity of the hüzün that Istanbul caused me to feel as a child, I must describe the history of the city ... the way this history is reflected in the city's 'beautiful' landscape and its people" (Pamuk 304).

For Pamuk, hüzün is not simply sadness; it is a shared mood of loss and longing, born from the city's ruins and faded grandeur (Pamuk 298–305). It is felt in crumbling wooden mansions, broken fountains, shuttered streets, a sorrow that glimmers with beauty. This matches your image of Istanbul as a necklace of pearls: each pearl shines with both grief and remembrance, each shimmer a piece of the city's layered memory.

Assmann notes that cultural memory becomes a "canon of the remembered," shaping not only what is recalled but also what is allowed to be remembered (Assmann 35). In Istanbul, this canon is visible in the mosaics of Hagia Sophia, which still glow faintly beneath layers of dust; in the walls of Topkapı Palace, whispering of sultans and secrets, and in the Grand Bazaar, where spices, copper, and voices mingle, each stall holding fragments of untold stories. These are not only material remains but carriers of memory. To walk in Istanbul is to walk inside a living archive. Every dome, every courtyard, every shimmering curve of the Bosphorus holds centuries within it. Forgetting here does not erase; it reshapes. Here Dr. Parui's statement can be aptly incorporated, to him remembering and forgetting are often operative not as ontological opposites but as structural and functional entanglements. (Parui 725) Memory and forgetting are like two strands of the same necklace, shining differently under the light. As Ricoeur reminds us, together they form our ethical task: to decide what we carry forward (Ricoeur 23).

However, Istanbul is not only a city of stone and water, but also a city of memory. It is a city that breathes through its people, whispers through its ruins, and glimmers with stories that refuse to end. To walk through it is to touch time itself, to hold both past and present in your hands, and to feel the city alive, forever remembered, forever luminous. Memory in Istanbul is both fragile and enduring. As Jan Assmann rightly observes, cultural memory transforms lived experience into collective stories, rituals, and symbols, allowing communities to maintain dialogue with their past (Assmann 118). In the same vein in Istanbul, this dialogue is not confined to archives or libraries; rather it is inscribed into streets, monuments, and public spaces. Byzantine mosaics, inscriptions on Ottoman mosques, and even modern graffiti are traces of remembering and forgetting. Forgetting here does not signify absence; rather, it forms another layer in the city's palimpsest, accommodating new narratives while preserving the traces of the old ones.

The layering of memory has both aesthetic and social significance. Discovering a forgotten courtyard or noticing a centuries-old fountain evokes both wonder and a subtle ache. Paul Ricoeur emphasizes that memory is never fixed; it is shaped by imagination, selection, and narrative interpretation (Ricoeur 23). In Istanbul, human memory interacts with the city's topography, creating a dense network of experience that spans centuries. Henri Lefebvre's insight that urban space is socially produced and carries both personal and collective significance resonates here very clearly. (Lefebvre 34).

Along the Golden Horn, natural history and human history converge in striking fashion. Fossils embedded in the banks, alongside centuries-old wharfs and mosques, produce a temporal layering that is almost tangible. The convergence of geological and human memory creates a cityscape where history is not only observed but lived and felt, reminding the observers that time flows in overlapping currents rather than a single line. The act of recalling in Istanbul is inseparable from forgetting, which functions both as constraint and enabler. Streets are rebuilt, alleys renamed, monuments reconstructed, and neighborhoods transformed.

Forgetting, as Ricoeur points out, is not mere absence but an active process shaping the capacity to remember (Ricoeur, 48–50). Reconstruction or erasure may obscure some stories, yet simultaneously illuminate others. The city demonstrates that memory is dynamic, contingent, and socially negotiated, a process evident in how people interact with urban space. This argument can not be justified with out Aminatta Forna's statement, "Forgetting is the best way to remember." (Forna 29) Public spaces like the Grand Bazaar exemplify the living nature of cultural memory. The aromas of spices, the echoes of footsteps, and the rhythmic cadence of trade connect present experience with centuries of urban practice. Assmann emphasizes that cultural memory exists not only in texts or monuments but in "the minds of those who inhabit shared spaces" (Assmann 118). Each interaction, conversation, observation, trade, reinforces the city's mnemonic continuity.

Historical memory is not a static display here; it is actively enacted, reinterpreted, and relived by generations of participants. The significance of Istanbul's layered memory extends beyond aesthetic appreciation; it shapes social identity and urban consciousness. The city holds multiple temporalities simultaneously, allowing residents and visitors to experience history as present, tangible, and dynamic. Memory in Istanbul fosters a sense of belonging, continuity, and responsibility toward the past, where streets, monuments, and neighborhoods serve as living archives of cultural Experience. Istanbul's monuments and urban topography serve as more than historical markers; they are active sites of memory that shape how people inhabit spaces. Minarets, domes, and arches are not merely architectural forms but locations of social memory, holding the echoes of rituals, political events, and community practices. Walking through Sultanahmet or across Galata Bridge, one experiences layers of memory encoded in material space. Each street corner, each fountain, and each courtyard carries histories that are continually reinterpreted, reminding residents and visitors that the city's memory is as much lived as it is recorded.

Daily life in Istanbul actively sustains this memory. Children playing on cobblestones, vendors negotiating in bazaars, and families observing old customs in public squares all participate in cultural memory. This living practice transforms the city into a continuous dialogue between past and present, where historical consciousness is embedded in routine movements, sensory experiences, and social interactions. In this sense, memory in Istanbul is inseparable from human experience: the city itself becomes a chronicle, where space, social action, and history converge to produce an urban consciousness that is constantly evolving yet deeply rooted in its past.

Ultimately, Istanbul stands as a living intersection where memory, forgetting, and urban space converge like threads in an intricate tapestry. The city's streets, courtyards, and monuments are not inert relics but vessels of collective experience, each layer of stone and shadow carrying stories that demand recognition and reflection. Here, memory is enacted in daily life, through the rhythm of marketplaces, the echo of prayers over rooftops, and the quiet persistence of centuries-old rituals, reminding observers that forgetting is never total and remembrance is never static. To move through Istanbul is to navigate a city that speaks simultaneously in past and present, a reinscription of human endeavor where history is continually rewritten and urban consciousness is constantly renewed. In this way, the city itself becomes a chronicle, a living manuscript in which each step, each glance, and each interaction threads another pearl into the luminous necklace of its enduring memory.

Cities narrate themselves in forms other than speech, inscribing meaning in architecture, streets, and the rhythms of daily life. Their stories are etched into stone, whispered along streets, and folded into the shadows of domes and arches. Among such cities, Istanbul stands as a living manuscript, a layered archive where time, memory, and human experience converge. To walk its streets is to encounter not just structures but echoes of lives long past, to feel history in motion, and to witness the interplay of absence and presence across centuries.

Topo imagination is the instrument through which Istanbul narrates itself. It does not simply observe the city; it inhabits it, perceiving layers of experience that ordinary vision cannot. Each street corner, mosque, fountain, and courtyard is a repository of memory, waiting to be read through imagination as well as observation. Henri Lefebvre asserts that space is socially produced, imbued with meaning by human activity and perception (Lefebvre 34).

Topo imagination makes this production legible, allowing urban space to convey the presence of past lives, the echoes of vanished neighborhoods, and the residue of human hope and despair that survives centuries.

Memory, in this framework, becomes tactile, audible, and performative. Jan Assmann observes that cultural memory transforms lived experience into symbols and narratives, creating continuity across generations (Assmann

118). In Istanbul, the concept of topo imagination allows one to feel the tension between continuity and rupture: the laughter of children on ancient stones, the sighs of a marketplace where traders once called across stalls, the quiet ache of streets demolished or displaced. These are not abstractions; they are living imprints, tangible and emotional, persisting through the city's topography. History, too, is inseparable from topo imagination. Paul Ricoeur emphasizes that memory reconstructs the past through narrative, shaped by imagination and choice (Ricoeur 23). In Istanbul, this reconstruction occurs constantly as the city interacts with its inhabitants. A domed mosque does not simply exist in isolation rather it enacts centuries of devotion, politics, and social life. A fractured fountain does not merely mark time; it witnesses the cycles of human need and generosity.

Topo imagination animates these traces, revealing how forgetting is never total, but layered, allowing some stories to resurface while others lie beneath, waiting to be rediscovered (Ricoeur 48–50). In walking through the city, topo imagination becomes a mode of empathy. It allows one to sense both joy and sorrow embedded in space, from the grandeur of Topkapı Palace to the shadows of narrow alleys where ordinary life continues against the backdrop of centuries. Each space carries fragments of human labor, memory, and imagination, threaded into a cohesive urban consciousness. Assmann notes that cultural memory survives in the minds of those who inhabit spaces and perform rituals, not merely in archives (Assmann 122). Here, topo imagination allows observers to inhabit the city's memory, experiencing it not as static history but as a living, participatory force.

Preservation is not the act of freezing time; it is the art of teaching walls to breathe again. Architects measure, draw, and plan. But preservers listen. They lean against cracked walls and hear prayers murmured into the plaster; they run their fingers across chipped tiles and feel the pulse of forgotten artisans. In Eyüp, a fountain stands in the shade of a plane tree where its marble is fractured, its inscriptions are fading, but for centuries it offered water to travelers, lovers, beggars, and poets. To restore it is not to polish it into something new, but to allow its voice to be heard once more. In his imagining, memory is not passive, rather it becomes an architecture, a sensual cartography where creation and preservation intertwine like ardent lovers, inseparable in their breath, immortal in their embrace.

Thus, Istanbul emerges as a living palimpsest, brought to life through the concept of topo imagination. Memory threads its way through the city's stones, streets, and shadowed corners, while history bends and refracts across every arch, fountain, and winding alley. Imagination weaves these layers together, forming a dynamic and coherent narrative where the city speaks through both presence and absence. Every attentive observation, act of preservation, or engagement adds a luminous brick to Istanbul's enduring monument of memory, each glimmer resonating with the weight of centuries. In this sense, topo imagination is simultaneously a method and a mode of experience, it teaches the city to articulate its histories, allows the past to unfold within the present, and reminds us all who traverse its spaces that memory, history, and imagination are inseparable forces, shaping the consciousness of Istanbul across generations.

Istanbul: A Tapestry of Memory and Continuity

The task of preservation is not to efface the scars of history but to render them legible—to allow fissures to speak in their own idiom. One might imagine an urbanism in Istanbul wherein every new structure bends to the contours of its antecedents rather than severing them: tramlines curving gently alongside mosques, towers ascending yet leaving interstices for courtyards where ancient mulberry trees still extend their shade. Such a vision is not reducible to nostalgia; it constitutes an *architecture of continuity*, a mode of inhabiting time through space. The Bosphorus itself offers this lesson: memory, like water, resists enclosure. Each wave bears sedimented fragments, the scent of fish grilled in Karaköy, the fleeting shadows of ferries traversing between Asia and Europe, the dissolution of the muezzin's call into the cries of circling seagulls. The strait has borne witness to imperial ascents and collapses, reflecting with equal fidelity the opulence of palaces and the fragility of shantytowns. Its melancholic cadence poses a critical question: can one envision a city in which the waterscape remains a commons, promenades accommodating both new lovers and elderly fishermen, and glass towers standing not as erasures of wooden piers but as coexistent witnesses within a shared temporal field? This is the praxis of *topoimagination*: a spatial ethics that insists upon designing without obliterating, building without silencing an urban poetics where continuity, memory, and futurity coalesce in the same topography.

To touch a stone in Istanbul is to touch the weight of centuries. The worn steps of Galata carry the echoes of merchants bearing silk, sailors dreaming of faraway ports, and exiles weeping at their departures. Even the tram that rattles along İstiklal Avenue, though modern in form, moves with a rhythm that belongs to the past. To encounter such spaces is to enter what Paul Ricoeur describes as the fragile balance between memory and forgetting. Not everything can, or should, be preserved; yet too much loss risks breaking the bond between city and citizen. What must endure are enough traces to keep despair from overwhelming belonging, enough fragments that future generations may still feel, through stone, street, and sound, the deep human longings that shaped the city into what it is.

A city without memory is only stone; a city with memory is a living soul. Istanbul shows us that memory is not static but layered, like pearls strung one after another, each reflecting light differently yet belonging to the same thread. Preservation here is not about clinging to ruins; it is about reimagining them as anchors of life. For instance Balat's colorful houses, in Sultanahmet's vast courtyards, and in the marketplaces where vendors still call out as if centuries have not passed, we see that urban planning can honor both fragility and resilience. To preserve without breaking, to build without erasing, is to honor the city's pulse. And so Istanbul loops back on itself, like a strand of pearls endlessly circling. Each story opens into another: the café that stands where a caravanserai once did, the apartment block that still holds the foundations of a Byzantine cistern, and the modern bridge that frames the silhouette of Ottoman mosques at dusk. To walk the city is to live its thunder of emotions, grief and wonder, despair and renewal, longing and love. It does not let us stand still; it pulls us into its folds again and again, reminding us that beauty lies not in perfection but in continuity, not in demolition but in care. To preserve Istanbul is to preserve the dwellers, it's fragility, the memory of the residents, and their desire to endure.

Istanbul has endured the sweep of centuries, yet it reveals itself in fragments, in whispers that curl around the curious, and in gentle nudges for those willing to pause. Its streets do not hurry; they insist on attention. Each neighborhood is a chapter etched in stone, every building a keeper of secrets, every alley a vein pulsing with the remnants of lives long vanished. The city is a living palimpsest, layers of emperors and traders, of longing and imagination, of dust and devotion, pressed into its marble, its plaster, and the worn cobbles that bear the footprints of countless generations. To move through Istanbul is to touch the pulse of history itself. One can hear the laughter of children long gone, still dancing across the thresholds of leaning houses, feel the weight of prayers that cling to minarets and arches, sense the quiet ache of lovers whose names dissolve into the wind. Every corner holds a memory, a shuttered balcony that trembles with the memory of a sigh, a fountain that murmurs the hopes of travelers who drank from it centuries ago. The city mourns, but it does not surrender. It holds the broken tiles and cracked stones as testaments, not tragedies, weaving the lives of the past into the breath of the present. Istanbul does not simply stand; it remembers. It hums with stories, aches with absences, and sings with shadows of joy and grief alike.

As the central argument of this book, Urban planning, when guided by understanding and reverence, need not be a hammer that silences these voice but it can be a gentle hand, weaving the new into the old, like a poet adding a line to an unfinished verse that has already endured centuries. A new structure can rise not by forcing the past into shadow but by entering into a conversation with it, tracing its own forms alongside the contours of memory, and acknowledging the weight of what has stood there before. Imagine a modern edifice bending lightly beside an ancient dwelling, sunlight threading between them like a bridge, shadows rippling over façades that have borne witness to generations of footsteps, whispered dreams, and long-forgotten songs.

The city, then, does not grow by obliteration; it grows by attunement, an intimate dialogue between the solidity of stone and the transparency of glass, between history and possibility, and between memory and imagination. Each addition becomes a subtle echo, a respectful gesture, and an acknowledgment that time itself cannot be hurried or erased but remembered in multiple forms. The past lingers not as a relic but as a spectral companion, guiding the present toward forms that honor continuity, that allow life to flow across centuries without rupture. In such a city, architecture becomes more than structure; it becomes memory incarnate, a language of presence that allows both the old and the new to breathe in tandem, allowing inhabitants to feel the pulse of their collective past even as they inhabit the promise of the future.

When a new building rises beside an old one, it does not simply occupy space; it joins a conversation that stretches across decades, sometimes centuries. The walls of the new structure do not mute the old; they echo it, reflecting its rhythms, shadows, and textures. Light passes between them, falls in unexpected ways on façades that have grown familiar to generations, and in these moments, the city speaks in whispers of what once was, of what endures, and of what might yet become. Topo imagination turns architecture into poetry. Every street corner becomes a stanza, every arch a verse, every alley a line of intimate narrative, connecting lives across time. Residents do not merely walk these streets; they inhabit memories, trace the steps of those who came before, and sense the invisible presence of the past in the hum of their daily lives.

In this city, memory and imagination are inseparable from the physical forms of buildings. A house is more than stone; it is a repository of stories. A doorway is more than an entrance; it is a threshold of remembrance. A roof is more than shelter; it is a silent witness to decades of human passage. When a modern structure rises beside it, the imagination fills in the spaces between imagining the children who once played in its courtyard, the meals prepared over a flickering stove, the seasons that have passed quietly above its tiles. The city becomes a layered landscape of feeling as much as of matter, where time folds upon itself and the past, present, and future breathe together in the same streets. Walking through such a city, one cannot help but feel that the very air which reverberates with stories. Every archway holds echoes, every narrow lane cradles recollections. The mind reaches out to touch them, connecting invisible threads between what was and what is, sensing patterns that defy simple observation. Topo imagination asks the observer to slow down, to see the city not as a collection of functional spaces, but as a living manuscript written in stone, plaster, and glass. Inhabitants are readers, architects are poets, and the city itself is both a story and a storyteller. It is a dialogue, endless and fragile, where the hum of daily life interweaves with the resonance of collective memory.

Even modern constructions do not impose; they resonate. A newly erected building with its glinting steel and reflective glass bends into the rhythm of the winding streets, its lines harmonizing with the timeworn houses beside it. Shadows stretch, mingle, and converse across walls that remember centuries, an unspoken dialogue between strength and endurance, novelty and memory. As Pamuk observes, "Istanbul was the city of my dreams, the city of my memories, the city of my imagination" (Pamuk and Freely 3). These words capture the essence of the previously discussed concept of topo-imagination, the capacity to perceive a city as both lived and remembered, where every step is an act of engagement with a layered past.

The city remembers the sultans and merchants, the teachers and seamstresses, the lovers and the lonely, all living together across centuries. One imagines a blacksmith hammering in a workshop now replaced by a modern shopfront, the rhythmic clang mingling with the distant drone of a car engine. One imagines a child running through a courtyard now occupied by a café, their laughter rising through the ages. Topo imagination makes these layers visible, not with the eyes alone, but with the heart, with the memory of the body as it moves through space. Even in decay, the city is alive. A crumbling wall, overgrown with ivy, speaks more than a polished glass façade. It carries the weight of the past, the carelessness of time, the persistence of life despite neglect. And the new structures, built beside it, do not shame it; they honor it by being present, by coexisting, by listening. Moreover, Urban planning becomes an act of empathy, the ability to imagine not just how people move through space, but how memory, history, and imagination inhabit it. Each street, each house, each shadow is a note in a symphony that plays quietly, persistently, for those who are willing to hear. Urban planning here is a careful hand, a balcony added without tearing down a centuries-old house, a roof extended without silencing the voices trapped in its timbers. The city advances not by conquest, but by dialogue, weaving the new into the old as if the present itself were learning to listen the silenced past in its architecture.

Bridges arch over water that carries more than ferries; it carries gossip, grudges, and the occasionally drowned hope. The Bosphorus remembers every tide that has kissed its shores, every argument shouted in the wind, every hurried promise made and broken. And in the alleys, the scent of freshly baked bread lingers alongside the distant, insistent call to prayer, while the laughter of children echoes from courtyards that no longer exist, as if mocking the absurd persistence of memory. Even here, where water meets stone, new structures emerge a small terrace overlooking the river, a narrow walkway climbing beside an old wall, designed to honor the past rather than flatten it. Planning becomes a form of storytelling, an architectural negotiation, proving that cities can grow without erasing the lives that already live within them.

To walk these streets is to feel centuries pressing beneath your feet, weighty but not cruel, like an old partner in crime reminding you of every mistake you ever made. Time is not a straight line here; it folds, twists, and sometimes trips over itself. Imagination wanders through streets alive with what was, what is, and what will almost certainly disappoint you tomorrow. And yet, new structures nestle in the folds, an attic here, a staircase there, without obliterating the stories that came before. It is not maps that matter, nor plans, nor the meticulous lines on paper that humans so desperately cling to. It is the city itself speaking, the past huffing and puffing, the present striding arrogantly alongside, and your heart slowly learning that to create, to preserve, to grow without destruction, is a lesson far more difficult than walking.This is Istanbul, always Istanbul, a city that refuses to simplify itself for your convenience. History is not politely behind you, nor neatly ahead; it folds into every corner, every wall, every streak of sunlight that falls between old and new. Urban planning here is an act of reverence, a careful arch added over a centuries-old alley, a modern doorway painted to complement an ancient façade, a new room that peers respectfully over a courtyard heavy with memory. It is poetry in motion, yes, but also a story full of irony, mischief, and the occasional smirk from a minaret that has seen far too much. The city remembers everything, forgives almost nothing, and allows the reader, careful, patient, a little foolish, to discover, sometimes with horror, sometimes with delight, that memory lives in space, imagination lives in memory, and even in the act of building anew, the past can be honored without compromise.

  Istanbul, the city that wears its history like armor and hides its secrets in the folds of every minaret and alley. Even the minarets seem to lean toward you conspiratorially, as if whispering secrets that the wind refuses to carry too far. Sunlight slips over cracked domes, illuminating the shadows that cling stubbornly to ancient walls, shadows that have witnessed empires rise, markets collapse, lovers vanish, and thieves disappear without a trace. Cobblestones murmur beneath your feet, each one hiding a memory: a merchant's hurried escape, a soldier's misstep, a poet's stolen kiss. And yet, amid the echoes of the past, new structures creep quietly forward. A glass-walled terrace appears where a courtyard once hid children's games; a narrow staircase wraps around a centuries-old alley. Urban planning here is not about erasure; it is a negotiation, a promise whispered between old walls and new ambition. The aim of any urban planning should not be to erase the past, rather it should learn to tiptoe around it, to add without disturbing, to create a conversation between the centuries.

Neighborhoods such as Karaköy exemplifies the ongoing conversation between past and present. Graffiti sprawls over centuries-old walls, sometimes irreverent, sometimes intimate, yet always conversing with the material traces of earlier life. Modern interventions, glass-walled studios, polished cafés, and renovated terraces do not erase the city's history. Rather, they enter into dialogue with it. Here, the aim of urban planning is not a linear march toward the new but a careful negotiation across time. Staircases wind around aged balconies, passageways thread through hidden courtyards, and terraces rise with awareness of the footprints that came before. Memory, imagination, and necessity coexist, layered within the city itself. To traverse Istanbul is to engage in a practice of memory-mapping, where invisible histories are translated into spatial experience. Every hilltop, every ferry crossing, even the quietest lane, invites reflection on lives that preceded the observer. Domes, mosques, caravanserais, and marketplaces converse with contemporary structures, producing a skyline in which past and present coexist visibly and audibly. The city's rhythms, the laughter of children, the hum of trade, the occasional silence of abandoned courtyards, interweave with architectural forms, transforming Istanbul into a living palimpsest. Here, memory is active, navigable, shaping perception and experience, inviting imagination to map the invisible onto the tangible.

This synthesis of memory and space speaks volumes with contemporary scholarship on urban imagination, where cities are read as repositories of collective experience and arenas for negotiation between continuity and transformation (Çakmak 112). Istanbul exemplifies this dynamic, remembering and reshaping simultaneously, insisting that those who traverse it remain attentive to the layers of human life embedded in its architecture. Ultimately, Istanbul manifests what can be understood as topo imaginatary, a spatial embodiment of memory, history, and imagination. Time is not displaced by modernity; it persists, layered across streets, terraces, and courtyards, accessible to anyone who observes, questions, and reflects. In this sense the urban planning must be carefully and mindfully done to preserve the memory and the imaginary space it inherits. This concept shall be discussed in the upcoming chapter.

In the heart of Istanbul, where the Bosphorus meets the land, the Hasanpaşa Gasworks stood silent for decades. Built in 1892 during the Ottoman era, it once illuminated the streets of Kadıköy with its coal gas. But as time passed, the world changed, and so did the needs of the city. The gasworks ceased operation in 1993, and the grand industrial structure was left to fade into obscurity. Yet, even in its abandonment, it tells stories of a bygone era, of craftsmanship, of a city in constant flux. Istanbul does not merely exist; it records, accumulates, and converses silently with every passerby. The Hasanpaşa Gasworks offers a vivid illustration once an industrial hub, now transformed into Müze Gazhane, it demonstrates how memory and adaptation coexist, where remnants of labor and fire converse with contemporary culture. Beyond singular examples, the city's urban fabric, from narrow alleys to grand palaces, holds collective memory, shaping everyday experience and human perception.

Istanbul's history is tactile, written in stone, brick, and iron. Every dome, bridge, and weathered wall carries traces of labor, devotion, and loss. Walking through the city is akin to navigating an archive, where topo imagination allows observers to read subtle inscriptions embedded in the built environment. A courtyard is never merely a courtyard; it embodies generations of conversations, footsteps, and silences. A mosque is never merely a mosque; it holds layers of ritual, politics, and collective memory accumulated over centuries. Topoimagination emerges here as a key lens. Every urban fragment, from decaying warehouses along the waterfront to lively market squares, participates in an ongoing dialogue between past and present. Adaptive reuse, restoration, and careful urban intervention are not neutral acts; they interpret memory, translating it into contemporary relevance while preserving historical resonance.

Urban memory carries a moral dimension. It is not simply historical; it is social and ethical. Neglecting memory erases human experience, whereas engaging with it thoughtfully enriches both residents and visitors. Müze Gazhane exemplifies this principle, its transformation does not romanticize decay but respects the labor, sound, and energy of the past while creating spaces for contemporary cultural activity. Memory, in this sense, becomes a guide for creativity, allowing the city to evolve while sustaining continuity.

The city of Istanbul carries its history in layers that cannot be erased; it retains memory in its stones, walls, and streets. The Hasanpaşa Gasworks, standing in Kadıköy since 1892, is an example of this embedded urban memory. Once a coal-lit industrial hub, it powered the neighborhood with light and energy during the Ottoman era. By 1993, the furnaces fell silent, leaving behind structures that spoke of labor, smoke, and fire. For decades, the site remained abandoned, a material witness to the city's industrial past. The transformation of Hasanpaşa Gasworks into Müze Gazhane (completed in 2021) demonstrates a contemporary approach to urban memory. The Istanbul Metropolitan Municipality, guided by architects and historians, preserved the industrial skeleton while integrating modern interventions. Glass, steel, and open spaces coexist with the brick and iron framework, allowing the building to serve a new cultural purpose without erasing its history. Architect Hasan Kalyoncu emphasizes that "adaptive reuse is a creative strategy that aims at preserving historical buildings and giving them a new use, making them suitable for present needs while keeping cultural value intact" (Kalyoncu 2024). In this sense, architecture becomes a dialogue between past and present, and the city's memory is made tangible through thoughtful design.

As the central objective of this book, Orhan Pamuk's novel *Istanbul: Memories and the City*, frequently reflects on how urban space embodies memory: the city a layered record, which documents personal recollections and collective history. Pamuk observes that Istanbul is a "city of stories" where the past continues to inhabit streets, squares, and buildings (Pamuk 17). Through this lens, the concept of topo imagination is very crucial since it preserves a city not only in its material forms but in the memories it becomes. A closer analysis might reveal that Urban planning which engages with topo imagination respects these layers of memory, be it adaptive reuse, preservation, or careful restoration of the city. Each building, plaza, or neglected ruin holds the potential to communicate the experiences of those who came before, offering a continuity that is both physical and cultural. Müze Gazhane is a prime example: it transforms industrial ruins into a space where contemporary life can coexist with historical memory.

    The city's history is never static. It is palimpsestic, layered with traces of empires, markets, and private lives. To navigate Istanbul attentively is to participate in the dialogue between past and present. History does not constrain the city but offers resources for creativity and resilience. Adaptive urban strategies can sustain the city's cultural energy while accommodating change, allowing memory to inform contemporary use.

    Ultimately, Pamuk captures this interconnection in his portrayal of Istanbul, reminding us that to engage fully with the city is to recognize the inseparable relationship between memory, history, and lived space . Topoimagination allows us to read this city as a mosaic of human experience. It is not merely about preservation but about interpretation, understanding how the footprints of the past shape contemporary life. A rusted furnace, a faded fountain, or a crumbling archway becomes a testament to continuity: a space where labor, devotion, commerce, and domestic life converge across centuries. Modern interventions, glass galleries, restored halls, or open courtyards, do not erase these traces; they illuminate them, creating a dialogue between what once was and what now is.

In this interplay, Istanbul teaches that history is not a static museum but a living presence. The city's memory manifests in subtle details: the uneven stones of a bridge, the weathered calligraphy on a mosque, the lingering scent of spices in a marketplace. Observing these signs, one feels the passage of time not as loss but as accumulation, where each layer enriches the one beneath. There is a quiet catharsis in recognizing this: an understanding that human lives, efforts, and imaginings are never entirely lost, and that the present is inseparable from the traces of the past. Istanbul's contemporary reality, with its bustling traffic, modern towers, and vibrant neighborhoods, does not diminish memory; it amplifies it. The past informs how people inhabit the city, how they negotiate space, and how culture persists in the interplay of old and new.

Through topo imagination, the city becomes a living archive, a continuous narrative where one can sense the presence of centuries without seeing them directly. It is in this fusion of history and present, memory and imagination, that Istanbul offers its deepest lesson that cities are not merely built but lived, remembered, and reinterpreted, and that human experience, when read attentively, can transform ruins into repositories of resilience, reflection, and enduring connection.

Works Cited

- Cakmak, A. S., et al. *Structural Analysis of Hagia Sophia: A Historical Perspective. Soil Dynamics and Earthquake Engineering*, vol. 3, WIT Press / Transactions on the Built Environment, 1993.
- Forna, Aminatta. *The Memory of Love*. Bloomsbury, 2010.
- Freely, John. *Istanbul: The Imperial City*. Penguin Books, 1998.
- Kalyoncu, Derya. "Spatial Narratives and Memory in Contemporary Istanbul." *Journal of Urban Cultural Studies*, vol. 7, no. 2, 2021, pp. 115–128.
- Lefebvre, Henri. *The Production of Space*. Translated by Donald Nicholson-Smith, Blackwell, 1991.
- Nora, Pierre. "Between Memory and History: Les Lieux de Mémoire." *Representations*, no. 26, 1989, pp. 7–24.
- Parui, Avishek. *Memory, Identity and the Colonial Encounter in India: Essays in Criticism*. Routledge, 2022.

Chapter-3

Restoring Memories Through Urban Planning

This chapter undertakes a critical examination of the ways in which urban planning can serve as a conduit for the restoration and reactivation of historical memory. Drawing on illustrative examples from Istanbul, India, and other global contexts, it interrogates how spatial design, architectural conservation, heritage-oriented urban interventions and memory-sensitive planning contribute to the reclamation of collective memory within the evolving urban fabric. This chapter argues in what ways global urban ideologies seek to modernize without entirely abandoning local memory with an intent to restore/preserve collective memory. Moreover, it will cite examples of already existing urban buildings that are constructed in the same pattern to restore memory. Among the city's (especially Istanbul's) most enduring monuments, the *Hagia Sophia* exemplifies this continuity through transformation. This chapter will discuss more such examples.

Originally conceived as a Byzantine basilica and later converted into an Ottoman mosque, it symbolizes not a loss of identity but an accumulation of cultural meaning. As,

Ahmed and Ahmad (2022) explain, its structural evolution demonstrates how architecture can act as a meeting point between civilizations, uniting aesthetic innovation with spiritual function. Moreover, the massive central dome, once described by Nur and Özer (2017) as a "golden cloud" suspended above light, illustrates the sophistication of early Byzantine engineering and its influence on Ottoman spatial design.

    Istanbul occupies a singular geographical and cultural position, straddling the boundaries of Europe and Asia and functioning for centuries as a bridge between contrasting civilizations. Its architectural landscape very distinctly reflects this dual identity, where Byzantine domes, Ottoman courtyards, and modern steel structures coexist within a single continuous urban fabric. This coexistence is not merely visual but historical; every district of the city reveals layers of political authority, religious expression, and artistic innovation. The built environment thus becomes a physical record of encounters between empires and ideologies, showing how geography, trade, and faith have collectively shaped Istanbul's evolving character. Rather than representing static periods of rule, the city's architecture demonstrates an ongoing negotiation between inherited forms and emerging technologies, revealing a continuity that defines its urban identity. Istanbul stands as a city unlike any other, bridging Europe and Asia through both geography and history. Its architecture expresses this dual identity, where religious monuments, civic structures, and modern developments collectively reveal the layered transformation of urban form. As Yüksel Burçin Nur observes, the city's-built environment functions as a "palimpsest of civilizations," a surface continuously rewritten through successive empires while preserving traces of earlier forms (2017). This description effectively captures how Istanbul's landscape reflects continuity amid transformation, where Roman foundations, Byzantine engineering, and Ottoman artistry coexist seamlessly within the fabric of a modern metropolis.

Another historical instance which stands nearby can be the Blue Mosque that portrays the refined geometry and exquisite surface design. Commissioned by Sultan Ahmed I, its cascading domes, tile-lined interiors, and slender minarets reflect the synthesis of spatial grandeur with ornamental detail. Together, these structures illustrate the city's capacity to absorb transformation without losing continuity; each new layer acknowledges the presence of the former, converting architectural adaptation into an act of cultural remembrance. Peter Heller (2022) argues that its design fuses the "spatial ideals of the Hagia Sophia with the ornamental richness of Ottoman artistry," illustrating how architectural memory can evolve into new creative expressions without severing historical lineage. Through this dialogue between imitation and innovation, the mosque becomes a continuation of the city's architectural conversation across eras.

Equally emblematic is the Topkapi Palace, the administrative and ceremonial heart of the Ottoman Empire. Designed as a self-contained city within walls, the palace integrates courtyards, gardens, and pavilions in a carefully ordered sequence that embodies political hierarchy and ritual precision. Each courtyard transitions from public to private domains, reflecting the gradual movement from imperial authority to domestic sanctity. The architecture's restrained ornamentation and spatial rhythm communicate the empire's ideals of harmony, discipline, and divine order. When examined together with the Hagia Sophia and the Blue Mosque, the palace completes a triadic narrative of Istanbul's past, a sacred devotion, artistic refinement, and imperial governance rendered visible through a structured form. As a matter of fact, the Topkapi Palace, reminds the contemporary generation about the residence of Ottoman sultans, the legacy of a political realm. A UNESCO (2019) report describes its courtyards and chambers as embodying "the imperial vision of the Ottoman world, where politics, ritual, and beauty were inseparable." This observation underscores that in Istanbul, architecture was not only limited to structural utility; but also communicated hierarchy, governance, and ceremonial order. The palace's layered spaces, public courtyards, administrative halls, and private chambers, translate imperial ideology into architectural rhythm, reinforcing how built form and political symbolism were historically intertwined.

Across the same skyline, new architectural interventions, bridges, cultural centers, and high-rise complexes stand beside centuries-old mosques and palaces, generating a visual dialogue between a lost memory and restored architecture. This juxtaposition reveals that Istanbul's urban identity is not determined by replacement but by coexistence. The transparency of glass façades reflects and reframes the silhouettes of domes and minarets, transforming the city into a living conversation between eras. As the prime argument of this chapter, modern planning initiatives emphasize connectivity and accessibility, yet they continue to operate within a terrain already inscribed with memory. As architecture theorist Sibel Bozdoğan notes, Istanbul continually negotiates between modernization and heritage, allowing new forms to participate in rather than erase the city's historic texture. The result is a spatial narrative that remains both globally relevant and locally resonant, a city where history is experienced not as nostalgia but as an enduring structural presence. (Bozdogan 89)

This coexistence defines Istanbul, a city where history is not confined to museums or ruins but lives that breathe alongside the future. As Sibel Bozdoğan (2001) explains in *Modernism and Nation Building*, the modern city of Istanbul is shaped by "a negotiation between memory and modernity," where new forms participate in, rather than replace, the historical fabric.(Bozdogan 53) This approach demonstrates that modernization in Istanbul operates through integration, linking technological progress with historical consciousness. The city's evolving skyline thus becomes a visible record of time itself: an architectural narrative that unites architecture, politics, and modern expressions into one coherent urban identity.

Istanbul: Restoring Memory through Art, Architecture, and Urban Space.

Istanbul is a city where memory is not static but constantly renewed through its art, architecture, and urban life. The Digital documentaries by TRT world rightly illustrates, the city's identity, rooted in its position across Europe and Asia, embodies a continuous dialogue between history and modernity. Once known as Byzantium and later Constantinople, Istanbul's layers of Roman, Byzantine, and Ottoman heritage form a living archive of artistic and cultural memory. This process can be understood through several mechanisms of memory preservation. Commemoration in planning is evident in Istanbul's architectural preservation; monuments such as the Hagia Sophia and the Basilica Cistern serve as memorials to ancient civilizations, where adaptive reuse has transformed sacred and civic structures into shared spaces of history. The Hagia Sophia, once a church and later a mosque, now serves as a symbol of coexistence and cultural continuity (Nur and Özer 2017). Hagia Sophia's structural and aesthetic innovation particularly its suspended dome, emphasizes advanced engineering and artistic integration of the Byzantine period and later inspired Ottoman design. A closer analysis can reveal that reintegration of marginalized spaces is evident in projects like the restoration of Ottoman hammams, including the Zeyrek Çinili Hammam, where traditional baths are reimagined as museums of everyday life, reconnecting the local community with forgotten rituals and crafts. Similarly, the Istanbul Modern Museum reclaims the city's industrial waterfront, reintegrating art into spaces previously isolated from the public realm. Through designing for memory restoration, Istanbul's landscape functions as a palimpsest, where contemporary structures deliberately echo the past. From the glass towers that mirror the domes of the Blue Mosque to public art installations that reinterpret Ottoman motifs, the city's structure expresses a deliberate remembrance through urban design. Bozdoğan's work on modernism and nation-building is worth mentioning in this this context as he explains that Istanbul's recent urban development operates through negotiation between historical memory and modernization, ensuring that new architecture participates and replaces the past. These layers reflect the architecture's narrative of continuity and transformation. Finally, participatory planning plays a growing role in Istanbul's cultural renaissance. The rise of community-led art fairs, open-air exhibitions, and heritage walks illustrates how citizens actively participate in shaping collective memory. As the Digital documentaries by TRT world explains, art here serves as both remembrance and resistance, a means of engaging with the past while envisioning an inclusive future. In essence, Istanbul exemplifies a city that restores memory not through nostalgia but through creative reinterpretation. Its skyline, where ancient domes converse with modern towers, becomes a metaphor for how the past and present coexist, shaping a vibrant and evolving cultural identity.

Hidden Dimensions of Istanbul's Artistic Legacy

Istanbul's artistic legacy extends far beyond its monumental skyline. Beneath the surface of its domes and minarets lies a layered continuum of cultural memory, where antiquity converses with the modern world. The city's museums and restored heritage sites stand as silent storytellers, preserving fragments of civilizations that once flourished along the Bosphorus.

Among these treasures, the *Alexander Sarcophagus* remains one of the most remarkable examples of artistic synthesis. Though not the true tomb of Alexander the Great, it features one of the rare portrayals of the conqueror created during his lifetime. The sculpture's striking realism and faint traces of original pigment challenge the long-standing myth that classical art was confined to colorless marble. Here, the vibrancy of ancient craftsmanship reclaims its rightful place in the continuum of artistic expression.

Equally evocative is the *Basilica Cistern*, where two colossal Medusa heads, repurposed as column bases, blur the line between mythology and materiality. Contrary to romantic interpretations, their placement was guided not by mythic reverence but by architectural pragmatism. This 6th-century reuse of Roman fragments reveals an early form of sustainable construction and creative adaptation, an architectural philosophy that finds resonance in contemporary restoration practices.

The recently restored *Zeyrek Çinili Hammam* deepens this dialogue between past and present. Within its walls, thousands of Ottoman tile fragments were unearthed, each one a fragment of memory and aesthetic devotion. Together, they reconstruct the sensibilities of Ottoman artisanship, its rhythm, color, and geometry, reviving the city's forgotten decorative language. Through such discoveries, Istanbul does not merely preserve its past; it reanimates it, turning archaeology into an act of storytelling.

Modern artists have continued this legacy of remembrance through reinterpretation. For example, the painter Osman Hamdi Bey infused native themes with European techniques, portraying introspection, scholarship, and self-awareness within richly detailed interiors. His art reflects the intellectual awakening of the late Ottoman period, a search for harmony between tradition and modernity. Likewise, Fahrelnissa Zeid, one of the first Muslim women to gain global recognition, transformed Islamic geometric forms into modern abstraction. Her vast, luminous canvases embody Istanbul's twentieth-century identity: hybrid, restless, and radiant with contradiction. Together, these artistic encounters demonstrate that Istanbul's heritage is not frozen in time. It evolves through cycles of loss and renewal, remembrance and reinvention. Restoration, reinterpretation, and creative innovation ensure that memory remains a living presence, woven through the stones, tiles, and brushstrokes of the city itself.

Urban Continuity: The Soul of the City

The concept of urban continuity in Istanbul is intricately bound to the city's historical architecture, serving as a tangible record of centuries of cultural and spatial transformations. This continuity is not simply about the preservation of buildings but embodies a collective recognition of the endurance of the city's material and spatial heritage. The Byzantine legacy, most prominently represented by monumental structures such as Hagia Sophia and the Church of Chora, establishes a foundational layer of architectural memory, where soaring domes, intricate mosaics, and ancient masonry articulate both aesthetic grandeur and historical depth. Overlaying this are Ottoman contributions, including Topkapi Palace, Sultan Ahmed Mosque, and the network of Ottoman-era residential streets, whose courtyards, narrow lanes, and interconnected domes reinforce patterns of spatial intimacy and continuity across centuries.

Districts such as Sultanahmet, with its dense concentration on historic mosques and palaces, and Galata, with its medieval towers and commercial streets, exemplify the coexistence of multiple historical layers, where the past remains materially and perceptually present within everyday urban life. Similarly, neighborhoods like Fener and Balat, with their crumbling mansions and restored synagogues, reveal processes of decay and renewal that underscore the city's resilience. Even infrastructural elements such as the Galata Bridge or the aqueducts of Valens serve as functional and symbolic links to the past, integrating historical consciousness into the urban fabric.

Through these architectural vestiges, Istanbul's urban continuity becomes legible not merely as an aesthetic or nostalgic phenomenon but as an operative framework through which residents experience the city. Narrow streets, hidden courtyards, and monumental domes mediate the perception of time, enabling the city to sustain multiple temporalities simultaneously. In this sense, Istanbul's built environment operates as a living archive, where continuity is enacted through the layering of Byzantine, Ottoman, and vernacular forms, each contributing to a durable, evolving urban identity. The endurance of these structures transforms the city into a vessel of cultural memory, allowing historical consciousness to inform both the material and experiential dimensions of urban life without hindering contemporary growth and adaptation.

The Architectural Chronicle of Constantinople

The history of Constantinople, now Istanbul, unfolds as an architectural palimpsest tracing the ambitions of successive empires. Founded as Byzantium around 660 BCE and reborn as Constantinople in 330 CE under Emperor Constantine, the city became a crucible of Roman, Byzantine, and Ottoman worldviews (Bayraktaroglu and Öktem Erkartal 31). The transformation of the city from Byzantium to Constantinople under Emperor Constantine was a deliberate act of imperial vision, signaling the city's strategic and symbolic importance in the Roman and Byzantine world. Kaya similarly underscores the continuity and adaptation of urban forms, showing how successive rulers shaped the city not only as a political capital but also as a spatial and cultural expression of power. Together, these works illustrate that Istanbul's architecture is more than a collection of buildings; it is a material record of imperial objectives, ideological shifts, and historical layering, where every structural addition, from fortifications and churches to palaces and mosques, encodes the priorities and identity of its ruling authorities. This perspective positions the city as a living topography, where the traces of earlier civilizations remain legible within the fabric of later constructions, enabling scholars to read the ambitions and legacies of empires through the urban landscape.

The *Hippodrome*, once capable of holding 100,000 spectators, symbolized imperial spectacle and civic unity (Volait and Avcıoğlu 112). The *Theodosian Walls*, with their triple fortifications and massive towers, represented a synthesis of art and engineering, protecting the city for nearly a millennium (Durusoy Özmen 582). The Hippodrome, as cited by Volait and Avcıoğlu, was far more than a venue for chariot races; it functioned as a central stage for imperial authority and civic engagement. Its immense capacity to hold 100,000 spectators illustrate not only the scale of Byzantine urban planning but also the integration of social, political, and cultural life within a single architectural space. The Hippodrome acted as a focal point where citizens and rulers intersected, reinforcing a shared sense of identity and collective experience within the urban fabric.

Similarly, the Theodosian Walls, highlighted by Durusoy and Özmen, exemplify the sophisticated convergence of art, engineering, and defensive strategy. Their triple layers of fortification, punctuated by massive towers, demonstrate a deliberate architectural response to both military exigencies and aesthetic considerations. The walls' ability to safeguard the city for nearly a millennium underscores the effectiveness of Byzantine urban defense while simultaneously shaping the spatial and symbolic boundaries of Istanbul. Collectively, these structures reflect a historical consciousness embedded in the city's architecture: monumental spaces like the Hippodrome facilitate social cohesion and performative display, whereas fortifications like the Theodosian Walls assert permanence, resilience, and continuity across centuries.

As briefly discussed earlier, Hagia Sophia, however, represents the pinnacle of Byzantine architecture. Built in 537 AD by Emperor Justinian I, its massive dome, supported by innovative pendentives, revolutionized the language of sacred space. Mango and Necipoğlu describe the dome's ethereal suspension above an ocean of marble and light as creating a spiritual geography beyond architectural form. Although its shape has changed over time due to earthquakes and repairs, the symbolism of the union of heaven and earth remains consistent. When Sultan Mehmed II entered the city in 1453, the Hagia Sophia became a mosque, its mosaics concealed yet preserved beneath Islamic ornamentation (Goodwin 94). The Ottoman architects, led by Mimar Sinan, absorbed its spatial logic into their own creations, the *Süleymaniye Mosque* and *Topkapi Palace*, infusing Islamic architecture with Byzantine grace. (Sev and Başarır

Figure 1. Hagia Sophia, Istanbul. Photograph by Sami Aksu, 2023. Courtesy of the photographer via Pexels.

22) Thus, Istanbul's skyline emerged as a seamless dialogue between faiths and forms, a continuity rather than a rupture.

Memory, Modernity, and Architectural Identity

The comparative tables presented below in this study are not only visual summaries but also analytical frameworks for understanding how architecture negotiates between memory and modernization. By aligning Istanbul's spatial evolution with parallel examples from India's capital Delhi, Newyork, Odisha's capital Bhubaneswar, Hiroshima (Japan) and Kashmir, this study situates Istanbul within a global discourse on *urban identity, cultural continuity, and architectural transformation.* Each case encapsulates distinct historical experiences yet converges on a common theme: the tension between preservation and progress. The following analysis explains in what ways memory is preserved with modern interventions and changes, and what are its impact on urban identity and planning.

City / Project	Architectural Memory Preserved	Modern Interventions/ Changes	Impact on Urban Identity and Cultural Memory
Bhubaneswar, India – Heritage Corridor Projects	Temple clusters, traditional street alignments	Pedestrianization, modern lighting, and landscape interventions	Reinforces spatial continuity and cultural identity; Architecture acts as a mediator of memory
Istanbul—Ottoman Heritage and Modern Renewal	Wooden houses, Byzantine cisterns, mosques, Hagia Sophia, Topkapi Palace	Glass towers, cultural centres, restored urban spaces	*Hüzün* reflected in juxtaposition of decay and renewal; memory persists through spatial layering and adaptive reuse
New York (Ground Zero)	Ruins and memorials of 9/11	Skyscrapers, museum complexes, public spaces	Contestation of memory in urban redevelopment: Architecture mediates grief, memory, and commercial pressures

| Hiro-shima Peace Park | Memorials, ruins preserved as reminders of atomic devastation | Parks, museums, and civic planning are integrating modern urban life | Architecture balances trauma, resilience, and public memory; spatial design fosters reflection and continuity |

Table 1

Istanbul, a Living topography of Memory and Modernization

The comparative table 1 functions as a critical analytical matrix rather than a mere descriptive summary. It elucidates how different cities across the world Bhubaneswar, Istanbul, New York, Hiroshima mediate the dialogue between architectural memory and the imperatives of modernization. Each entry reveals how urban landscapes embody a dynamic negotiation between historical preservation and contemporary intervention, thereby shaping distinct cultural and emotional geographies.

In the capital of Odisha, Bhubaneswar, the preservation of temple clusters and traditional street alignments within the Heritage Corridor Projects exemplifies how sacred spatial memory is sustained through modern infrastructural sensibilities such as pedestrian pathways and aesthetic lighting. Architecture here becomes a conduit of cultural continuity, mediating between the past's sacred aura and the present's civic functionality.

Istanbul, conversely, emerges as a palimpsest of civilizations where Ottoman wooden houses, Byzantine cisterns, and monumental structures like Hagia Sophia coexist with glass towers and urban restorations. The city's landscape evokes *hüzün*, a melancholic sense of collective memory that endures through the layering of decay and renewal, demonstrating how adaptive reuse becomes an act of remembrance.

New York's Ground Zero epitomizes the contestation of memory within the capitalist urban order. The interplay between ruins, memorials, and skyscrapers transforms architecture into a mediator of grief and resilience, reflecting the city's struggle to balance commemoration with the imperatives of redevelopment and commerce.

In Hiroshima, memory assumes a moral and spatial dimension. The Peace Park integrates preserved ruins with modern civic planning, creating a site where trauma and renewal coexist. Architecture here becomes an ethical landscape fostering reflection, reconciliation, and the continuity of collective memory. Through this comparative lens, the table underscores a shared global tension the effort to preserve the mnemonic essence of cities even as they evolve under the pressures of modernization. Architecture, in each context, operates as both archive and agent: preserving memory while scripting the future of urban identity.

Istanbul exemplifies this through restored Ottoman houses and Byzantine cisterns juxtaposed with modern glass towers, creating a skyline that mirrors the city's *historical layering*, a visible dialogue between preservation and modern transformation. The urban landscape of Istanbul reveals a continuous negotiation between history and modernity. Across the city, carefully restored Ottoman residences and Byzantine underground structures coexist with contemporary glass and steel skyscrapers, forming a skyline that embodies temporal depth. This visual contrast does not suggest conflict rather a peaceful dialogue between endurance and change, where architectural memory is woven into the progressive modernization. In this way, Istanbul becomes a living archive, allowing the past to persist even as the city redefines itself through new architectural languages.

Authenticity vs. Reconstruction:

Post-war reconstruction in Warsaw and Berlin demonstrates how accurate reconstructions of historic quarters preserve spatial memory while incorporating modern necessities. Similarly, Hagia Sophia and Topkapi as discussed earlier retain their original materials and spatial hierarchies, alongside structural reinforcements. This emphasizes the continuity of spatial hierarchies, where the arrangement of courtyards, domes, and internal chambers preserves the intended experience and flow of the original designs. Here, it is imperative to acknowledge that it further underscores the role of engineering reinforcements, which have allowed these structures to withstand natural decay, earthquakes, and successive modifications without compromising their historical integrity. Together, these studies demonstrate that preservation in Istanbul is not merely about conserving visible surfaces; it involves safeguarding the conceptual and experiential essence of the architecture, allowing both the material and spatial dimensions of these historical sites to communicate the city's enduring cultural memory.

Extending this argument further, the Political agendas and Urban Symbolism of Hiroshima and Newyork's Ground Zero demonstrate how architecture mediates collective trauma and projects national narratives. As in Istanbul,

Ottoman and Republican interventions in urban heritage reflect shifting political and religious priorities, in the same vein Commercialization of Memory and adaptive reuse of the originally dilapidated materials like stone, bricks in Delhi and Hiroshima highlight how commercial pressures coexist with heritage preservation, where architecture acts as a bridge between memory, identity, and contemporary urban life. Memory in these above-mentioned cities reveals how modern urban growth continually negotiates with the traces of its past. In these cities, adaptive reuse, the transformation of old buildings into new cultural or commercial spaces, becomes a language through which history survives within modernity. Rather than existing as static relics, historical structures are reinterpreted and repurposed, allowing them to function as living archives of collective identity.

Old/New Delhi-

Another significant aspect concerns India's capital, Delhi. *Old Delhi's tradition and heritage*, originally named Shahjahanabad, is a quintessential example of Mughal urban planning. Its narrow lanes, bustling bazaars, and intricately carved havelis preserve the aesthetic and social life of centuries past. Courtyards served as communal spaces, while arched gateways and jharokhas reflected artistry and attention to detail. The material palette, red sandstone, wood, and lime, emphasized local resources and craftsmanship, creating spaces rich in cultural memory. The examples of Old Delhi and New Delhi illustrate a similar but chronologically distinct spatial transition. Old Delhi, originally Shahjahanabad, represents an architecture of cultural intimacy and social continuity. Its narrow lanes, central courtyards, and Mughal havelis reflect localized craftsmanship and materiality, red sandstone, wood, and lime, that connect community life to architectural space. Each element functions as a mnemonic device, linking the sensory and social dimensions of lived experience. In contrast, New Delhi, designed by Edwin Lutyens in the early twentieth century, translates colonial ambition into urban form. Broad boulevards, administrative axes, and monumental structures such as the Rashtrapati Bhavan and Parliament House embody order, control, and visual dominance (Sharma 78). The architectural language of New Delhi marks a decisive break from vernacular tradition, privileging function and authority over the embodied memory of place.

When read in parallel with Istanbul, Delhi as a city illuminates a shared dynamic, the negotiation between cultural rootedness and modern ambition. Istanbul's post-Ottoman urban planning, like Lutyens' modernist grid, reflects global design ideologies that sought to modernize without entirely abandoning local memory. Yet Istanbul differs crucially in intent: where New Delhi imposed a new order upon an existing landscape, Istanbul's modernization integrates old and new within a single evolving fabric. Its mosques, cisterns, and restored districts stand beside glass façades and bridges, forming a spatial continuum rather than an architectural rupture (Volait and Avcıoğlu 118). Thus, Delhi's architectural dichotomy explains how Istanbul balances its historical self-image with the necessity of urban progress and why its skyline embodies both nostalgia and innovation, a harmony that New Delhi's monumentalism often resists.

Traditional Kashmiri houses are an integration with nature. Traditional Kashmiri homes ('Kothis') feature wooden structures with sloping roofs and intricately carved balconies. They are climate-responsive and harmoniously integrated with the surrounding landscape. The use of local timber and mud bricks reinforced cultural identity while supporting sustainable living practices (Pandit 102). These homes mirror the same principle seen in Old Istanbul houses, where architecture is intertwined with daily life, climate, and social practices. The inclusion of traditional and modern Kashmiri houses extends the argument from metropolitan planning to domestic architecture. Traditional Kashmiri homes, constructed with wood, mud brick, and carved balconies, represent an architecture deeply responsive to geography and climate (Pandit 102). Their spatial organization, with courtyards and sloped roofs, integrates human habitation into the rhythms of the natural environment. By contrast, modern Kashmiri residences made of concrete and steel reflect a global trend toward standardization and functional uniformity (Koul 56). These structures prioritize durability and cost-efficiency but often neglect the cultural and aesthetic dimensions that once defined Kashmiri identity. The shift from vernacular to industrial materials parallels Istanbul's own evolution, from wooden Ottoman houses to glass-and-steel high-rises, where globalization introduces a homogenizing aesthetic that risks displacing local architectural character.

This comparison demonstrates why Istanbul's approach to modernity remains distinctive. While both regions adapt to contemporary demands, Istanbul's architecture consciously reinterprets the past rather than discarding it. Adaptive reuse projects, such as the transformation of Ottoman hammams and the establishment of the Istanbul Modern Museum, reflect a deliberate effort to sustain cultural continuity within modern urban life (Bozdoğan 2001). The transformation of historical structures through adaptive reuse represents not merely an act of preservation but a dialogue between the past and the present. In Istanbul, projects such as the conversion of Ottoman hammams and the creation of the Istanbul Modern Museum exemplify how architectural memory is reinterpreted within the discourse of modern life. These sites, once rooted in the social and cultural fabric of the Ottoman city, are not frozen relics of history; they have been reimagined to serve contemporary urban needs while retaining the essence of their historical identity. By reusing spaces that once embodied collective rituals of community and culture, Istanbul sustains a tangible link with its layered past. The hammams, symbols of social intimacy and urban unity, now function as cultural venues or design spaces, extending their role from cleansing the body to nourishing collective memory. Similarly, the Istanbul Modern Museum situates modern art within a historically resonant industrial site, demonstrating how heritage can evolve rather than vanish.

Such transformations illustrate that continuity in Istanbul's urban identity lies not in resisting change but in absorbing it meaningfully. As Bozdoğan (2001) observes, these acts of reuse bridge temporal divides, allowing history to breathe within modernity. The city thus becomes an active archive, where architecture speaks the language of its past while participating in the narratives of the present. In this sense, Istanbul exemplifies an urban consciousness that recognizes architecture as both heritage and instrument of renewal.

Then Mughal havelis turned into cafés or Ottoman warehouses converted into art galleries embody the dual condition of preservation and commodification. The stones that once bore witness to imperial rituals now participate in urban economies, selling not only goods but curated experiences of nostalgia. This shift illustrates how architecture mediates between *memory* and *market*, translating cultural continuity into a form that aligns with contemporary urban desires. Yet, as Durusoy Özmen (583) and Kaya note, this coexistence is not without tension. While adaptive reuse preserves physical heritage, it also risks transforming memory into a commercial spectacle where history is consumed rather than remembered. In this sense, architecture becomes both a bridge and a battleground: a bridge connecting past identities with present needs, and a battleground where authenticity and profit contest the meaning of heritage. Ultimately, the adaptive reuse of space in Delhi and Istanbul mirrors the cities' memories , the topographies of civilizations constantly rewritten by commerce, culture, and time. Through this lens, memory is not merely stored in stone; it is performed, negotiated, and, at times, sold.

This observation emphasizes how historic buildings are not only preserved as static relics but are actively integrated into the dynamics of contemporary urban life. In both Delhi and Istanbul, adaptive reuse demonstrates that commercial pressures, such as tourism, retail, and real estate development, do not necessarily undermine heritage; instead, they can coexist with preservation efforts in a way that sustains the cultural and historical significance of the architecture. By converting old palaces, havelis, or Ottoman-era mansions into hotels, cafés, museums, or cultural centers, the built environment becomes a medium through which collective memory and local identity are continually enacted. Architecture, in this context, functions as a bridge: it links the city's historical narratives with present-day social and economic activities, allowing residents and visitors to experience memory tangibly while engaging with contemporary urban life. In effect, adaptive reuse transforms heritage structures into living participants in the city, reinforcing continuity of identity and memory even as commercial imperatives shape their form and function.

This coexistence reflects Istanbul's ability to restore memory through adaptation rather than mere conservation. Contemporary structures mirror domes, arches, and courtyards of Ottoman and Byzantine precedents, showing that the city's transformation is guided by historical consciousness. As Durusoy Özmen observes, this layering of spatial memory and modern functionality enables Istanbul to evolve without erasing its cultural substratum (Durusoy Özmen 583). This suggests that the city's historical structures and urban patterns are not static relics but active participants in shaping contemporary urban life. By maintaining and integrating Byzantine and Ottoman architectural elements alongside modern infrastructure, Istanbul preserves the traces of its past while accommodating present-day needs. The "layering" refers to how historical memory is embedded within the built environment-palaces, mosques, streets, and courtyards-allowing residents and visitors to perceive and interact with multiple temporalities simultaneously.

Modern interventions, whether in transportation networks, restored monuments, or urban redevelopment, do not completely overwrite these historical layers but coexist with them, creating a dialogue between continuity and change. In essence, Özmen highlights the city's capacity for adaptive resilience, where urban growth and modernization are harmonized with cultural preservation, ensuring that Istanbul's identity remains historically grounded even as it transforms. The process illustrates how memory operates as an active design principle in the city's urban development and why architecture here transcends function to become a vessel of identity.

Architecture and Cultural Memory: Reflections on Comparative Urban Examples

Architecture is not merely a functional construct; it is a vessel of collective memory, reflecting the social, cultural, and historical narratives of a city. Examining Istanbul's architectural evolution alongside cities like Delhi and regions like Kashmir provides insight into how urban transformations affect cultural memory and identity. The function of architecture is more than a utilitarian framework; it is a repository of collective memory and identity. Through its physical form and spatial organization, architecture embodies the social, cultural, and historical narratives that define a city's evolution. Each structure, from monumental mosques to modest dwellings, carries within it traces of the past, stories of continuity, adaptation, and transformation. The city, therefore, becomes a living archive where built forms act as tangible expressions of collective experience and cultural resilience.

When examined alongside other historical urban contexts, such as Old and New Delhi or the traditional and contemporary architectural transitions in Kashmir, similar patterns emerge. In these regions, the built environment reflects the negotiation between heritage and modernization. Delhi's colonial-era planning and post-independence urban expansion demonstrate how spatial reconfigurations can both preserve and alter cultural identity. Similarly, in Kashmir, vernacular wooden architecture rooted in climatic adaptation and craftsmanship continues to inform local identity, amidst modernization. Such comparative perspectives highlight that architecture is not merely about design or construction but about sustaining continuity across time. It anchors memory within space, linking communities to their histories while allowing room for transformation. Cities like Istanbul, Delhi, and Kashmir thus illustrate how architecture serves as a bridge between the past and the present, preserving identity while responding to evolving social, political, and economic realities. Through these layered architectural narratives, cultural memory finds enduring expression, ensuring that urban transformation does not equate to cultural erasure. The purpose of this chapter is to examine how architecture serves as a repository of cultural memory and a metaphor for the endurance of history within the modern city. It aims to trace how spatial forms, architectural imagery, and urban transformations are represented in the text (*Istanbul: Memories and the city*) as expressions of continuity, identity, and belonging. Through a close reading of the novel's depiction of Istanbul and a comparative consideration of other culturally layered spaces such as Delhi and Kashmir, this chapter explores how literature translates architectural and spatial realities into narrative memory. The discussion further seeks to understand how the intersections of time, space, and structure contribute to shaping the city's cultural identity, revealing architecture not merely as a backdrop but as an active narrative force that preserves and redefines collective memory. The juxtaposition of old and new in Istanbul mirrors patterns observed in Delhi and Kashmir: Preservation vs. Progress. Istanbul's contemporary landscape demonstrates that architecture, when interwoven with history, social practices, and materiality, becomes a living repository of memory and transformation. The city's *architectural continuity* arises from this tension between past and present, where every structure contributes to a historically layered urban identity.

Gurses (2010) interprets Pamuk's narrative as an articulation of Istanbul's liminal character, situated between the legacies of its imperial past and the pressures of modernity. The city's identity emerges as a palimpsest, where layers of historical memory coexist with contemporary cultural transformations, reflecting both its enduring heritage and its evolving urban reality.Gurses emphasizes that Istanbul is a city shaped by both its past and present. Its architecture and urban spaces show traces of earlier Ottoman and Byzantine periods while also adapting to modern styles. This layered character means that the city's memory and identity are preserved even as it changes over time. In scholarly terms, Istanbul acts like a living record of its history, where past and present coexist in everyday life and urban form. Istanbul's architecture reflects a complex dialogue between its historical past and the pressures of modern urban development. Over the course of many centuries,

Istanbul has undergone successive periods of architectural transformation, reflecting the successive dominions and cultural influences that have shaped its built environment. The Byzantine period contributed monumental structures, such as churches and fortifications, which emphasized both religious symbolism and civic power. The Ottoman era introduced grand mosques, palaces, and public complexes, integrating Islamic architectural principles with local craftsmanship. Later, European influences, particularly from the 18th and 19th centuries, brought new stylistic elements, such as neoclassical and baroque designs, which were incorporated into civic buildings and private residences. Together, these layers of architectural intervention have produced a complex urban fabric, where remnants of past eras coexist alongside more recent developments, allowing the city itself to function as a living record of its historical and cultural evolution (Bozdoğan 2001; Kuban 2010). Historic mosques, hammams, and houses stand alongside modern apartment blocks and contemporary cultural centers, showing how preservation efforts aim to maintain the memory of the past while accommodating contemporary needs. Scholars note that this coexistence of old and new allows the city to retain its cultural identity even as it modernizes, producing an urban fabric where heritage and modernity are intertwined (Yerasimos, 1990). This layered urban texture not only tells the story of Istanbul's historical transformations but also demonstrates how architecture can serve as a living archive of collective memory.

Feature	Old Delhi	New Delhi	Traditional Kashmir	Modern Kashmir	Istanbul
Materials	Red sandstone, wood	Concrete, steel	Wood, mud, clay	Concrete, glass	Stone, wood, glass
Design Philosophy	Ornamentation, symbolism	Monumentalism, order	Climate-Responsive, craftsmanship	Efficiency, standardizationst	Cultural fusion, adaptation
Cultural Reflection	Mughal heritage	Colonial legacy and traditions	Traditions	Global Influences	Byzantine and Ottoman heritage
Urban Layout	Pedestrian-centric	Grand Boulevards	Symmetrical, functional	Standardized layouts	Mixed, adaptive to topography

Table 2

This comparative table 2 functions as an architectural and cultural taxonomy that delineates how materiality, design philosophy, and spatial logic articulate distinct trajectories of memory and modernity across five urban contexts Old Delhi, New Delhi, traditional and modern Kashmir, and Istanbul. It maps the evolving dialogue between tradition and transformation, revealing how architecture, as both form and philosophy, becomes a vessel for cultural expression and historical consciousness.

In Old Delhi, the use of red sandstone and wood manifests as a tactile intimacy with history, On the other hand, its ornamental architecture highlights its saturation with Mughal symbolism and spiritual undertones. The pedestrian-centric urban layout reinforces the rhythm of lived memory, where narrow alleys and marketplaces preserve social cohesion and cultural continuity.

New Delhi, conceived under colonial imperatives, embodies a monumental geometry and order. Constructed in concrete and steel, its grand boulevards represent the rhetoric of empire discipline, hierarchy, and surveillance. Yet, its very rigidity also testifies to an imposed vision of modernity, one that juxtaposes the organic density of Old Delhi with the spectacle of planned power.

Traditional Kashmir, in contrast, reflects an architecture born of environmental wisdom and artisanal craftsmanship. The use of wood, mud, and clay situates its buildings within the valley's ecology, emphasizing climate-responsiveness and cultural rootedness. Its symmetric and functional layout is an aesthetic of balance between nature and habitation, memory and utility.

Modern Kashmir, however, translates this intimacy into efficiency. With concrete and glass replacing traditional materials, and standardized layouts overriding vernacular rhythm, the region's architecture marks a rupture where modernity's uniformity threatens to dissolve the artisanal ethos that once defined Kashmiri identity.

Interestingly Istanbul emerges as a city of synthesis, a living topography of Byzantine, Ottoman, and global influences. Its architectural language fuses stone, wood, and glass, embodying a cultural hybridity that is both historical and contemporary. The city's urban planning philosophy of adaptation mirrors its topography and its layered history, rendering Istanbul an emblem of how memory and modernity can coexist through spatial negotiation.

Collectively, this comparison illuminates the ways architecture materializes memory while responding to the shifting aesthetics and politics of modernization. Each city's form is not merely a built environment but an evolving narrative an archive of cultural endurance, adaptation, and transformation.

However it is imperative to note here that, this comparative reading reveals that Istanbul stands between preservation and transformation, combining the memory-laden human scale of Old Delhi and Traditional Kashmir with the technological modernity of New Delhi and Modern Kashmir. In Istanbul, urban continuity is neither static nor purely nostalgic; it operates through topographical layering, where architectural memory is inscribed, erased, and rewritten across time.

Through a comparative exploration of Istanbul, Delhi, and Kashmir, it becomes clear that architecture operates as a dynamic conduit between memory and modernity. Istanbul's ever-transforming urban fabric anchored by monumental sites such as the Hagia Sophia, the Blue Mosque, and the Topkapi Palace, yet redefined by glass towers and revitalized cultural spaces embodies a continuous negotiation between historical consciousness and contemporary imperatives. The comparative tables reveal how materiality, form, and spatial experience shape cultural identity across regions.

Thus, what these examples reflect is a shared concern with preserving identity within modern development; how they do so is through architectural layering, adaptive reuse, and community participation; and why they matter lies in their ability to sustain emotional and cultural continuity amidst rapid urban transformation. It is important to note that Istanbul's unique position at the intersection of continents and historical eras makes it both a living city and a symbolic representation of memory. The phrase *remembers through building* (One building; Four Empires 2023) suggests that Istanbul's architecture preserves layers of its past, mosques, palaces, and historic streets which act as tangible records of its cultural and political history (Bayraktaroglu and Öktem Erkartal 34). Simultaneously, the phrase *"builds in order to remember"* highlights the conscious effort to construct new spaces that honor or recall past traditions, showing how urban development itself can serve as a method of historical preservation (Koul 56). Together, these perspectives underline the city's dual role as a repository of memory shaped by centuries of human activity, and as an active participant in shaping collective memory through ongoing architectural and urban interventions.

Challenges and Tensions
Memory vs. Modernization

Hagia Sophia serves as a striking example of how architecture can embody the ongoing dialogue between historical memory and contemporary identity. Originally constructed as a Byzantine basilica in the 6th century, it symbolized the spiritual and political power of the Byzantine Empire. When it was converted into an Ottoman mosque in 1453, Islamic architectural elements such as minarets, mihrab, and calligraphic inscriptions were integrated, reflecting the city's new cultural and religious identity. In the 20th century, its transformation into a secular museum represented the modern Turkish Republic's effort to preserve historical heritage while promoting a neutral, civic identity. Today, as it functions again as a mosque, further interventions adapt the space for contemporary worship while maintaining its layered historical narrative. Each of these changes required careful architectural modifications that not only altered the building's physical form but also reshaped how people experience and interpret its history which is ingrained with their collective memory. (Necipoğlu 67; Volait and Avcıoğlu 118)

For example, during the Ottoman conversion of Hagia Sophia, architectural elements such as minarets, the mihrab, and calligraphic panels were introduced. These additions went beyond indicating a shift in religious function; they fundamentally altered the way the interior space was perceived and used. The minarets introduced a new vertical dimension, emphasizing height and creating visual connections with the surrounding cityscape. The mihrab directed the focus of worshippers toward Mecca, reorganizing circulation patterns within the hall. Calligraphic panels not only decorated the space but also conveyed religious and cultural identity, guiding the visual and spiritual experience of visitors. Later, when Hagia Sophia was transformed into a museum, interventions such as the installation of modern lighting, signage, and designated visitor pathways further reshaped the interior. These changes facilitated contemporary circulation and public engagement with the monument but inevitably modified how historical atmospheres were experienced. Each phase of modification demonstrates that the building's form is not static; it is continuously negotiated to balance the preservation of historical memory with the practical and cultural needs of successive periods (Necipoğlu 67; Volait and Avcıoğlu 118).

Hagia Sophia: An Architectural Memory

Hagia Sophia exemplifies the complex interaction between historical memory, religious identity, and political agendas in Istanbul's built environment. Constructed in the sixth century as a Byzantine basilica, it symbolized the authority of the Byzantine Empire, both politically and spiritually, with its monumental dome and expansive interior reflecting imperial power and communal cohesion. Following the Ottoman conquest in 1453, the building was converted into a mosque, and key architectural interventions, such as the addition of minarets, the mihrab, and large calligraphic panels, were introduced. These changes did not merely signify religious transformation; they actively altered spatial organization, circulation patterns, and visual hierarchies, integrating Islamic architectural principles while maintaining the underlying Byzantine structure (Necipoğlu 67). These modifications also reflected the Ottoman political agenda of asserting authority and demonstrating continuity between the city's imperial past and its new Islamic governance.

In the twentieth century, when Hagia Sophia was repurposed as a museum, further interventions were implemented to accommodate public access and heritage preservation. Adjustments in lighting, the introduction of designated visitor pathways, and protective installations were designed to manage large numbers of tourists while maintaining the integrity of the historic fabric (Volait and Avcıoğlu 118). These changes demonstrate how the building has been continuously adapted to reconcile historical memory with contemporary political, social, and cultural priorities. This negotiation mirrors broader trends in Istanbul's urban landscape. Old Istanbul architecture, including Byzantine and Ottoman monuments, traditional wooden houses, and narrow streets, preserves historical identity, local craftsmanship, and cultural continuity, often reflecting political and social hierarchies of the past. In contrast, contemporary developments, such as high-rise apartments, commercial complexes, and modern infrastructure projects, reflect the political and economic agendas of urban modernization, often prioritizing functionality, growth, and global visibility over historical preservation. From an architectural perspective, this juxtaposition highlights the tension between conservation and modernization: the city's historical core embodies memory, tradition, and identity, whereas new urban forms negotiate contemporary political, social, and economic imperatives. Hagia Sophia, through its successive transformations, epitomizes this dynamic, showing how Istanbul's architecture mediates between historical legacy, political intent, and the practical demands of the present, creating a layered and continuously evolving urban fabric.

    The global recognition of Hagia Sophia as a cultural and historical landmark has also introduced significant commercial pressures that further shape its architectural experience. Infrastructure such as visitor pathways, interpretive signage, and controlled access points inevitably influence circulation patterns and the perception of interior and exterior spaces (Bayraktaroglu and Öktem Erkartal 31). These interventions, designed to manage large crowds and facilitate interpretation, mediate how visitors engage with the architecture, often prioritizing visual spectacle and ease of movement over subtle spatial and material experiences. Practices such as large-scale photography, virtual tours, and media representation emphasize iconic features, including the central dome and Seraphim mosaics, which may overshadow smaller architectural details and nuanced spatial relationships. In this way, the commercial framing of Hagia Sophia actively participates in the ongoing negotiation between the preservation of historical memory and contemporary use, influencing both perception and material engagement with one of Istanbul's most significant architectural monuments.

Preservation of Memory-The need to renew without Erasing

Urban modernity often faces a paradoxical tension, the need/desire to renew without erasing. Across diverse geographies, contemporary urban planning increasingly embraces the notion that progress must cohabit with the mnemonic strata of place. Cities, once symbols of rupture, are now curated as living archives, where architecture negotiates between inherited form and emergent function. The conservation of historical urban sites whether through adaptive reuse, material continuity, or spatial reinterpretation embodies an evolving ethic of memory preservation. The cases of Mumbai's Dadabhai Naoroji Road Heritage Precinct, Jodhpur's Birkha Bawari Stepwell, and Seoul's

Seoullo 7017 Skygarden exemplify how modern design can reanimate the past without fossilizing it, translating memory into a civic and aesthetic resource.

Dadabhai Naoroji Road Heritage Precinct, Mumbai: Curating the Colonial Archive

Mumbai's Dadabhai Naoroji Road (DN Road) constitutes one of the most instructive examples of heritage-led urban management in postcolonial India. Originally planned in the late 19th century under the British Raj, the road was lined with neo-Gothic and Indo-Saracenic façades reflecting imperial grandeur. Over time, however, the precinct succumbed to visual clutter billboards, unauthorized signage, and infrastructural decay obscuring its architectural coherence and symbolic legacy.

Figure 2. Botev, R. (2023). *Dr. Dadabhai Naoroji Road, Fort (Mumbai precinct)* [Photograph]. Wikimedia Commons. Licensed under CC BY 3.0 P

The Heritage Streetscape Project (2003–2007), initiated by the Mumbai Metropolitan Region Heritage Conservation Society (MMRHCS), sought not mere restoration but the recontextualization of the precinct within the rhythms of a twenty-first-century metropolis. The project, guided by the conservation architect Vikas Dilawari, removed visual intrusions, standardized signage, restored façades, and improved pedestrian access while preserving the patina of age. The result was not a nostalgic reconstruction but a subtle urban choreography that allowed historical memory to coexist with contemporary function.

Here, preservation operated not as stasis but as curated continuity the recollection of colonial urban order transformed into a democratic urban space. DN Road thus exemplifies how heritage-led planning can reclaim historical streets as mnemonic corridors, enabling the collective to inhabit its past without being imprisoned by it. In Pierre Nora's terms, the site functions as a *lieu de mémoire*; a living "site of memory" that sustains identity through spatial experience rather than monumental reverence.

Birkha Bawari, Jodhpur: Reviving Water Memory through Ecological Design

In the desert city of Jodhpur, architect Anu Mridul's Birkha Bawari (2009) reinterprets the ancestral stepwell as a form of sustainable infrastructure. Historically, *bawaris* (stepwells) in Rajasthan served as both water reservoirs and communal gathering spaces, embedding hydrological intelligence within vernacular form. Modern urbanization, however, led to their neglect, severing the link between ecology, architecture, and cultural ritual.

Birkha Bawari reclaims this memory through an act of ecological remembrance. Designed as a 16,000-cubic-metre rainwater-harvesting reservoir for the Umaid Heritage Township, the project fuses traditional stepwell geometry with modern engineering. Local sandstone, hand-cut masonry, and stepped terraces evoke the archetypal Rajasthani form while integrating contemporary hydraulic systems. The architecture thus performs a dual task technological utility and cultural continuity.

The project transforms memory into a functional aesthetic: the recollection of water's sacred and social role becomes the template for sustainable urban design. As an intervention, Birkha Bawari demonstrates how the memory of form deeply rooted in environmental ethics can be rearticulated in the language of modern planning. The stepwell ceases to be an artifact and instead becomes a generative prototype for a future reconciled with its ecological past. It embodies what theorist Tim Edensor calls *"vernacular memory"* a mode of remembering material practices embedded in the everyday landscape.

Figure 3.OpenAI. "A Photograph Captures a Stepwell, Known as a Baori." *DALL·E*, 2025. AI-generated image.

Seoullo 7017, Seoul: Reclaiming Infrastructure as Urban Memory

Seoul's Seoullo 7017 Skygarden (2017), designed by the Dutch firm MVRDV, epitomizes the transformation of obsolete modernist infrastructure into a mnemonic urban landscape. The name "7017" symbolically fuses the year of the original overpass's construction (1970) with the year of its rebirth (2017), encapsulating five decades of urban metamorphosis.

The original Seoul Station Overpass, once a traffic artery, had become structurally unsafe and socially obsolete. Rather than demolish it, as a gesture of erasure the city reimagined it as a linear park, integrating 24,000 plants representing 228 local species. Each plant is labelled in Korean and Latin, creating a *botanical archive* that functions simultaneously as ecological restoration and cultural text. The project introduces pathways, cafés, and performance areas, transforming the alienating modernist viaduct into a participatory civic space.

Seoullo 7017 thus enacts memory through adaptive reuse, where infrastructure becomes an agent of reconciliation between Seoul's industrial past and its post-industrial aspirations. The elevated walkway overlooks the city's historical station and markets, visually layering temporalities within one spatial field. In doing so, it performs Michel de Certeau's notion of "spatial storytelling"; inscribing memory into everyday mobility and social interaction.

Importantly, Seoullo also reflects Seoul's broader policy of regenerative urbanism, which foregrounds sustainability, accessibility, and identity. The project's success lies not only in its aesthetic transformation but in its symbolic reversal: what was once a relic of vehicular modernity now fosters pedestrian intimacy and environmental renewal. The memory of concrete thus becomes the foundation of an urban ecology attuned to both past and future.

Figure 3. Shin, Kyungsub. "Seoullo 7017 Skygarden / MVRDV." *ArchDaily*, 22 May 2017, https://www.archdaily.com/ 872325/ seoullo-7017-skygarden-mvrdv.

Urban Memory as Design Ethic

Across Mumbai, Jodhpur, and Seoul, these interventions articulate a shared architectural philosophy memory as method. Instead of perceiving the city as a palimpsest to be overwritten, planners and architects have begun to read it as a text to be annotated. Whether through streetscape conservation, ecological reconstruction, or infrastructural reuse, memory operates not as nostalgia but as a critical continuity linking the ethical, environmental, and aesthetic dimensions of urban life.

Dadabhai Naoroji Road anchors the colonial archive within civic modernity; Birkha Bawari reclaims indigenous ecological wisdom; and Seoullo 7017 transforms industrial ruin into communal space. Each enacts preservation not as a backward gaze but as a forward strategy, transforming recollection into design intelligence. In doing so, they reaffirm the role of urban planning as a cultural practice of remembrance: a discipline that builds not merely with materials, but with time itself.

Frank Lloyd Wright: Memory, Continuity, and the Organic Ethic of Space

If the urban projects of Mumbai, Jodhpur, and Seoul demonstrate how contemporary design preserves memory through adaptation and renewal, then the architectural philosophy of Frank Lloyd Wright must find a mention in this context which provides the theoretical ground on which such continuity may be understood. Wright was an American architect and designer whose stellar architectural vision, though conceived in the early 20th century, remains profoundly relevant to present debates on heritage, sustainability, and the discourse of space. His notion of "organic architecture" an architecture that grows naturally from its environment and embodies the spirit of its inhabitants, renders him a precursor to the modern concern for memory as an architectural ethic.

For Wright, architecture was not an act of imposing form upon space but of *revealing* the essence latent within it. He famously declared, *"No house should ever be on a hill or on anything. It should be of the hill, belonging to it."* This intimate dialogue between structure and site articulates a philosophy of topographical empathy a way of building that acknowledges the geological and cultural memory embedded in landscape. In this sense, Wright's architectural language is not merely modernist; it is mnemonic. His buildings remember the land they occupy.

Figure 4. Daderot. *Fallingwater (Kaufmann Residence), by Frank Lloyd Wright*. 17 May 2013, Wikimedia Commons, CC0.

Organic Architecture as a Philosophy of Memory

Wright's organicism was more than aesthetic harmony; it was a moral stance against the fragmentation of modern life. The industrial age, he argued, had estranged man from nature, from craft, and from the authenticity of dwelling. His response was to envision buildings that could mediate continuity between past and present, human and natural, memory and innovation.

Wright's Structures, such as Fallingwater (1935) and the Unity Temple (1905) demonstrate how Wright materialized this idea. *Fallingwater*, suspended over a waterfall in Pennsylvania, fuses domestic space with the geological flow of the stream beneath. The sound of water permeates the interior, dissolving the boundary between nature and habitation. This integration creates what phenomenologist Christian Norberg-Schulz would later describe as *"a sense of place"*—an experience that situates human existence within the memory of its surroundings.

The Unity Temple, on the other hand, redefines the sacred in architectural modernity. Built with reinforced concrete then a radical material choice—it retains a meditative inwardness reminiscent of ancient sanctuaries. The use of indirect light, geometric order, and spatial enclosure invites what Martin Heidegger would call *"dwelling poetically"*, the act of inhabiting space as a mode of remembering one's being in the world. Thus, Wright's architecture can be read as a form of architectural phenomenology, anticipating the mid-20th-century theoretical concern with space as an existential and mnemonic category.

Architecture as Cultural Continuity

Wright's architectural vocabulary is steeped in the memory of indigenous American traditions and Japanese aesthetics, yet it resists mimicry. His engagement with Japanese architecture, particularly during his travels in the early 1900s, shaped his sensitivity to asymmetry, horizontality, and the continuity between interior and exterior. In this, he discerned a philosophy of impermanence and *wabi-sabi*—the beauty of transience—which deeply aligns with the notion of architecture as a living, breathing form of memory.

At the same time, his Prairie Houses (such as the Robie House, 1909) express the democratic ideal of a uniquely American architecture. Their low horizontal lines and open plans echo the vastness of the Midwest landscape while rejecting the vertical hierarchies of European urbanism. In these designs, Wright sought to translate geography into form, turning landscape into a symbolic language of cultural identity. The architecture remembers the land not through imitation, but through rhythm, proportion, and materiality.

This aesthetic of continuity parallels the memory-preserving ethos of projects such as the Dadabhai Naoroji Road restoration or Seoullo 7017, which reinterpret inherited spatial patterns within a contemporary matrix. Wright's insistence on local materials and contextual sensitivity anticipates what we now call critical regionalism—an approach theorized by Kenneth Frampton as the reconciliation between universal modernism and vernacular rootedness. In essence, Wright's architecture stands as a prototype for a heritage-conscious modernity—a design practice that constructs the future without erasing the past.

Memory as Ethical Architecture

Central to Wright's thought is the belief that architecture must embody moral integrity. Beauty, for him, was inseparable from truth and truth to materials, to environment, and to human need. His critique of imitation and ornamentation mirrored his ethical disdain for falsehood in culture. Architecture, he claimed, must "speak of its time and place, but yearn for timelessness." This yearning is the essence of memory in architectural form not a mere recollection of history but an aspiration toward continuity with it.

In the broader discourse of memory and urban planning, Wright's work provides a philosophical foundation for viewing architecture as a medium of remembrance. His organic buildings do not monumentalize memory through fixed commemoration; instead, they allow memory to flow through living space through the tactile presence of wood and stone, the play of light, the rhythm of movement. In this respect, his architecture aligns with the Birkha Bawari stepwell, where tradition becomes functionally reinterpreted, and with Seoullo 7017, where industrial heritage transforms into a civic landscape of renewal. All three operate under the same ontological principle: that memory must be lived, not displayed.

Modern Resonance and Legacy

Wright's vision resonates powerfully with twenty-first-century urbanism, where the challenge lies in crafting sustainable cities that honor their histories. His emphasis on organic integration, sustainability, and human scale prefigures today's ecological design movements. Moreover, his architectural storytelling—where form narrates its relationship to site offers a profound counterpoint to the placelessness of global modernism.

In contemporary projects like the High Line in New York or Seoullo 7017 in Seoul, we see Wright's legacy refracted: obsolete infrastructures reimagined as communal gardens, spaces that heal the rupture between memory and modernization. Likewise, the Dadabhai Naoroji Road heritage project echoes his spirit of contextual preservation, and the Birkha Bawari embodies his organic principles in an Indian idiom—reviving vernacular hydrology as a living architecture.

Through these parallels, one perceives how Wright's philosophy transcends temporal boundaries. His architecture remains a dialogue across time, an ethics of place-making that binds memory, material, and modernity into one continuous narrative. In reading Wright today, we are reminded that every city is both an artifact and an organism—its memory not frozen in monuments, but pulsing through the very rhythm of its renewal.

Heritage Impact Assessment: H I A

As urban landscapes evolve under the pressures of modernization, the delicate equilibrium between heritage preservation and developmental necessity has emerged as one of the central concerns of contemporary architectural ethics. In this context, the Heritage Impact Assessment (HIA) serves not merely as an evaluative instrument, but as a philosophical and methodological bridge between the past and the future an institutionalized framework through which the cultural memory of place is safeguarded even as cities undergo transformation. At its core, the HIA is a systematic process that identifies, predicts, and evaluates the potential effects of development projects on the *Outstanding Universal Value (OUV)* of heritage sites. Initially conceptualized within the ICOMOS and UNESCO World Heritage Centre frameworks, HIA extends beyond architectural analysis into the realm of cultural semiotics reading the urban landscape as a palimpsest of historical meanings, social practices, and collective memory. As such, it redefines preservation not as conservation in stasis, but as dynamic continuity, ensuring that development emerges as an extension rather than an erasure of inherited forms.

The Philosophical Basis of HIA: Memory as a Planning Paradigm

The underlying philosophy of HIA resonates deeply with the **mnemonic modernity** discussed in earlier contexts the stepwell of Jodhpur, the adaptive reuse of Seoullo 7017, or the restoration of Mumbai's heritage boulevard. Each of these interventions embodies the ethical premise that architecture is a repository of cultural memory. HIA formalizes this principle into a procedural discipline, transforming affective remembrance into measurable criteria of spatial impact.

From a theoretical standpoint, the HIA embodies what Pierre Nora calls *lieux de mémoire — sites of memory* where the material traces of the past persist as vessels of collective identity. However, unlike static heritage lists or conservation ordinances, the HIA introduces temporality into preservation, acknowledging that memory is lived, layered, and often contested. It requires planners and architects to engage with heritage as a living narrative, to interpret how proposed changes might recontextualize rather than destroy historical meanings embedded in space.

Aldo Rossi's notion of the *collective memory of the city* in *The Architecture of the City* (1966) provides a theoretical corollary: urban form, he argues, constitutes an archive of lived experience, and thus, any alteration to that form must be measured against its capacity to sustain this mnemonic continuity. The HIA, therefore, becomes both a technical and an ethical apparatus a means of protecting the *memory value* of place.

Methodological Structure: Mapping Tangible and Intangible Impact

Practically, an HIA involves several interrelated stages:

- **Baseline Documentation** – It establishes the heritage significance of the site, including tangible and intangible attributes;
- **Assessment of Potential Impacts** – It analyses how proposed interventions (construction, restoration, urban redevelopment) might affect these attributes;
- **Mitigation Measures** –It proposes design modifications or management plans that minimize adverse effects;
- **Monitoring and Adaptive Management** – It ensures that the site's integrity and symbolic coherence are preserved over time.

However, beyond these procedural dimensions, the contemporary relevance of HIA lies in its ability to translate cultural narratives into spatial policy. For example, the Dadabhai Naoroji Road Heritage Streetscape Project in Mumbai, often cited as a model of heritage-sensitive urban renewal, implicitly enacts the principles of HIA. The project's visual surveys, stakeholder consultations, and facade controls ensured that modernization (traffic management, infrastructure upgrades) did not rupture the colonial-era architectural rhythm that defines the street's historic character. The "impact" here is not only physical but experiential — preserving the memory of the urban promenade as a socio-cultural continuum.

Similarly, the restoration and reinterpretation of Birkha Bawari Stepwell in Jodhpur foreground the intangible dimensions of heritage impact. The project reactivates traditional water-harvesting practices while re-embedding them in a contemporary ecological discourse. An HIA of such a project would not only examine structural integrity but also evaluate how the intervention revives cultural knowledge systems, community engagement, and environmental ethics all of which constitute intangible heritage values.

HIA in Global Context: The Case of Seoullo 7017

The Seoullo 7017 Skygarden in Seoul provides one of the most emblematic global instances where HIA principles have guided an adaptive reuse project of infrastructural heritage. Transformed from an obsolete 1970s highway overpass into a pedestrian greenway, the project demonstrates how urban memory can be re-scripted through design.

Rather than demolishing the elevated structure a gesture that would have erased a tangible fragment of Seoul's post-industrial narrative planners chose to reinterpret it as a connective, human-centered landscape. The project underwent an extensive heritage and environmental impact analysis that assessed visual corridors, cultural sightlines, and neighborhood morphologies. The resulting intervention maintained the material memory of the overpass while infusing it with new social meaning. The HIA framework, here, operated as a lens through which heritage was redefined not as preservation of an obsolete form, but as continuity through transformation.

The Seoullo 7017 project thus embodies what HIA at its most evolved form aspires to achieve: *a choreography of coexistence* between the modern and the memorial, between the pragmatic logic of infrastructure and the symbolic logic of collective remembrance.

HIA as Cultural Ethics and Policy Instrument

In contemporary discourse, Heritage Impact Assessment is not confined to monumental or UNESCO-listed sites; it has evolved into a policy instrument for sustainable urban governance. The global guidelines established by ICOMOS (2011) advocate the integration of HIA into Strategic Environmental Assessments (SEA) and Environmental Impact Assessments (EIA), creating a holistic framework for evaluating development. The philosophical shift is significant, as heritage is no longer an aesthetic afterthought but a structural determinant of urban planning.

Moreover, HIA encourages public participation

and stakeholder consultation, recognizing that heritage significance is socially constructed and contextually interpreted. This participatory ethos aligns with the postmodern urbanism of inclusion seen in Istanbul's adaptive restoration movements and Seoul's community-engaged planning initiatives. The HIA process thereby democratizes heritage discourse, transforming architectural memory from elite curation into collective authorship.

From Assessment to Aesthetics: The Future of HIA

As cities like Mumbai, Istanbul, and Seoul grapple with the twin imperatives of modernization and preservation, the HIA must evolve from being a bureaucratic protocol into a creative interpretive practice. Architects and planners must learn to read impact not only in quantitative metrics such as visual intrusion or traffic flow but also in qualitative terms of cultural resonance and emotional geography.

To borrow from Andreas Huyssen, heritage in the global city functions as a *"present past"*—a temporal fold where memory inhabits modernity. The HIA, when applied with critical sensitivity, ensures that this coexistence is neither nostalgic nor destructive but dialogic. It demands that every new architectural gesture carries within it a consciousness of what has come before. In this sense, the HIA stands as both a technical and philosophical embodiment of the principle articulated through the works of Frank Lloyd Wright and echoed across the global heritage projects discussed earlier: that architecture, to endure meaningfully, must not only build upon the ground but also build upon memory.

In Istanbul, architecture is more than a physical construct; it is a layered chronicle of human ingenuity, cultural negotiation, and historical memory. Hagia Sophia, with its soaring dome, reinforced piers, intricate mosaics, and hierarchical spatial organization, stands as an enduring testament to this dialogue (Necipoğlu 67; Mainstone 143; Volait and Avcıoğlu 118). Every architectural intervention, whether the Ottoman addition of minarets and mihrab, the reinforcement of the dome after seismic collapses, or the subtle restoration of hidden mosaics, reflects a careful negotiation between structural necessity, aesthetic vision, and socio-political symbolism. The building is simultaneously a monument, a laboratory, and an archive, its stones whispering the ambitions, devotion, and artistry of successive civilizations.

Beyond Hagia Sophia, the city itself preserves fragments of forgotten architectural memory. Timber lattices of Ottoman houses, repurposed Roman columns in Byzantine cisterns, and centuries-old neighborhood mosques reveal patterns of domestic, civic, and religious life now hidden beneath modern façades (Kaya; Durusoy Özmen 583). The rediscovery of tile fragments, hidden inscriptions, and worn ornamental details during restoration projects illuminates techniques, materials, and design philosophies that were nearly lost to time. These elements, often subtle and overlooked, anchor the city's contemporary skyline in a deep architectural past, creating a continuum where history is tangible in every cornice, arch, and dome.

Modern interventions, glass towers, cultural centers, and restored institutions, do not erase the past but frame it, allowing historic and contemporary forms to coexist (Bayraktaroglu and Öktem Erkartal 34). Participatory urban planning ensures that restorations honor spatial integrity, materiality, and ornamentation, transforming architecture into a collective act of memory and identity. Through the interplay of stone, timber, steel, and glass, Istanbul's skyline becomes a living archive, where domes, courtyards, façades, and alleyways together narrate centuries of ingenuity, adaptation, and aesthetic dialogue.

Ultimately, Istanbul's architecture demonstrates that buildings are not static monuments but living entities, continually negotiating the tension between memory and modernity, authenticity and adaptation, and continuity and transformation (Volait and Avcıoğlu 118). In Hagia Sophia and across the city, every dome, every arch, and every hidden detail carries the trace of human skill and imagination. Architecture here is both witness and storyteller, preserving memory, shaping experience, and connecting past, present, and future in a tangible, spatial narrative that endures through time.

Istanbul's urban landscape is a living dialogue between its past and present, where architecture acts as both a vessel of memory and a canvas for modern aspirations. The city, historically Byzantium and later Constantinople, carries layers of Roman, Byzantine, and Ottoman influences that have shaped its spatial and cultural identity. Traditional architecture in Istanbul is characterized by human-scale proportions, the use of locally available materials such as timber, stone, and brick, and ornamentation that carries both cultural and symbolic significance. These architectural features were not only practical responses to climate and available resources but also expressions of social values and communal memory. Narrow streets, inward-facing courtyards, and multi-generational houses encouraged interaction within neighborhoods, while decorative elements, such as intricate woodwork, patterned tilework, and carved motifs, embedded narratives of local identity, religious practice, and shared history within the built environment (Çelik 2004).

In contrast, contemporary architecture in Istanbul increasingly prioritizes globalized aesthetics, large-scale construction, and commercial functionality. These new structures, while visually impressive, often disrupt the continuity of the city's historical fabric. The shift from human-scale streets and courtyards to towering glass-and-steel edifices exemplifies a tension between memory preservation and modernization (Kuban, 2010).

Istanbul's urban landscape embodies a rich and layered dialogue between its historical past and contemporary developments, where architecture functions both as a repository of collective memory and as a stage for modern aspirations. Historically Byzantium and later Constantinople, the city carries the marks of Roman, Byzantine, and Ottoman civilizations, which have shaped not only its physical layout but also its cultural, social, and symbolic identity (Çelik, 2004). Traditional Istanbul architecture demonstrates memory-preserving qualities in multiple dimensions. The choice of materials, stone, timber, and decorative tiles anchors buildings in the local environment, reflecting regional craftsmanship and techniques that have endured over centuries. The human-scale design of courtyards, narrow streets, and neighborhood-focused layouts fosters social interaction, communal cohesion, and a sense of belonging, embedding everyday life within a framework of shared memory. Decorative elements, including calligraphy, mosaics, and wood carvings, communicate cultural and religious narratives, integrating symbolic meaning into the very fabric of the city. Additionally, the thoughtful integration of natural elements such as gardens, fountains, and the city's proximity to the Bosphorus demonstrates a harmonious relationship between urban life and the surrounding landscape, reinforcing continuity and connection between the built environment and nature.

In contrast, contemporary architectural interventions increasingly emphasize a globalized aesthetic, favoring glass facades, steel frameworks, and large-scale constructions aligned with international design trends (Kuban, 2010). These modern structures, including high-rise towers and expansive commercial complexes, often dominate traditional streetscapes, transforming both the visual and social experience of the city. The functional focus of contemporary architecture frequently prioritizes commercial or economic needs over cultural or communal purposes. Many new buildings disregard local materials, climatic considerations, and historical patterns, which diminishes the continuity of Istanbul's historical fabric and interrupts the intimate scale and rhythms that characterize traditional urban life. This contrast highlights a persistent tension between preserving historical memory and accommodating modernization. Istanbul's memory-preserving features, materiality, scale, ornamentation, and integration with natural surroundings, exist alongside modern tendencies toward globalized aesthetics, monumental scale, and functional priorities. Together, they create a layered urban fabric in which past and present constantly negotiate their coexistence. Appreciating this complex interplay is crucial for understanding how

Istanbul's architecture not only reflects its historical and cultural identity but also shapes social interactions, urban experiences, and the city's evolving sense of place.

Implications in Urban Planning

The juxtaposition of old and new architectures reveals Istanbul's ongoing negotiation between memory and modernity. While historical buildings evoke a sense of nostalgia and continuity, modern constructions often generate a sense of temporal disconnection, revealing the contrast between inherited cultural forms and contemporary design (Çelik, 2004). Urban planners and architects face the challenge of balancing preservation with innovation, ensuring that Istanbul's evolving skyline does not erase the narratives embedded in its historic fabric.

In contemporary urban planning, memory plays a crucial role in shaping sustainable and culturally grounded cities. Istanbul demonstrates how traditional architecture preserves historical, social, and cultural memories, yet modern developments often disrupt this continuity. Memory-sensitive Urban planning emphasizes integrating heritage and historical context into new designs, ensuring that cities retain their identity while evolving (Çelik 45). Smart city technologies and digital archives further support this goal by documenting streetscapes, buildings, and communal narratives, allowing planners and citizens to engage interactively with urban memory (Graham and Marvin 78). Importantly, urban memory should be treated as **living memory**, not confined to static monuments; it thrives in adaptive spaces like repurposed heritage buildings, cultural centers, and public areas that blend historical significance with daily use, fostering active participation and continuous engagement with the past (Freely 112; Kuban 203). By combining memory-sensitive strategies, digital tools, and interactive living spaces, cities can create an evolving urban fabric that balances modernization with cultural preservation, ensuring that memory remains a dynamic, integral part of urban life.

Conclusion

Istanbul stands as a city where memory and modernity constantly meet, creating an urban landscape layered with emotion, history, and change. Its older quarters, marked by courtyards, domes, and narrow streets, continue to speak of a time when architecture was deeply tied to community rhythm and cultural expression. These places embody the idea that buildings can hold memory, not only through material form but through the shared experiences of people who lived within them. Yet, as new constructions rise across the skyline, tall, reflective, and globally styled, many of these memory-laden sites risk being overshadowed or erased. This shift reveals a pressing question in contemporary urban studies: how can a city expand and modernize without losing its narrative identity (Çelik 47)

Modern urban planning has begun to respond through what scholars call ***memory-sensitive design***, an approach that values continuity over replacement. This method promotes a balance where innovation is guided by awareness of the past. Integrating old street patterns, maintaining sightlines to historic monuments, or reusing traditional materials are not acts of nostalgia but ways of keeping cultural ecosystems alive. Technology now supports this effort in meaningful ways. Digital mapping, online heritage archives, and interactive databases record reinterpret the city's architectural memory. Smart city tools allow planners to analyze how communities use public space while preserving traces of older urban life. To Graham and Marvin ,When used thoughtfully, these technologies become extensions of memory rather than instruments of erasure (Graham and Marvin 81).

At the heart of this approach lies the concept of living memory, the idea that history should breathe within the present. Living memory transforms the urban environment into a space of dialogue, where past and present exchange meaning through participation.

Restored heritage buildings can serve as cultural centers, modern plazas can embed stories through digital projections, and citizens can interact with the city's layered history through augmented experiences. Such initiatives do more than preserve; they heal collective wounds, reconnecting residents to forgotten narratives and reclaiming urban spaces once marked by displacement or neglect. Restoring memory, therefore, is not about longing for a vanished world; it is about giving people the tools to understand where they come from and how their surroundings evolved.

On a serious note, when Urban planning embraces memory as a living process, it contributes to a more inclusive and humane city. As a matter of fact, Istanbul's evolving skyline can be read not as a conflict between old and new but as a shared story, one that acknowledges loss, continuity, and renewal. Through memory-sensitive planning, digital archives, and interactive architecture, the city can shape a future that honors diversity, fosters belonging, and turns memory into an active force for sustainability. The statement that urban planning is "an act of care" by Graham and Marvin becomes particularly meaningful when considered in the context of Istanbul. (Graham and Marvin 92) In this city, the preservation of physical traces of the past, such as Ottoman houses, Byzantine churches, narrow historic streets, and traditional marketplaces, serves as a critical link to centuries of cultural and social memory. These architectural elements are not simply decorative or functional; they embody the lived experiences, aesthetic sensibilities, and historical narratives of generations, anchoring the city's identity amidst rapid modernization.

Moreover, involving communities in these processes enhances the city's social cohesion. Residents, architects, and urban planners collaboratively shape the urban environment, interpreting heritage in ways that are meaningful for present-day life while safeguarding it for the future. In Istanbul, examples such as the adaptive reuse of Ottoman mansions, the restoration of historic hammams, and the careful integration of modern high-rise buildings along the Bosphorus illustrate how urban care can preserve cultural continuity while responding to contemporary pressures. Therefore, this approach transforms urban planning into a dynamic practice of cultural stewardship, one that balances the tangible and intangible layers of the city, ensuring that Istanbul's past remains an active and respected part of its present and future.

As a matter of fact, this chapter stands as a pivotal site for encapsulating and restoring the essence of any city or country. These spaces are not merely aesthetic or functional;

they are deeply intertwined with the lives, emotions, and histories of those who inhabit them. The chapter emphasizes that old architecture carries intrinsic value, reflecting centuries of social practices, artistic sensibilities, and spatial philosophies that modern urban forms often overlook. Its preservation is crucial not only for cultural continuity but also for maintaining the city's unique character, which distinguishes Istanbul from other metropolitan landscapes.

At the same time, the chapter critically examines the impact of new architecture, urban expansion, and contemporary design interventions on the city's historical fabric. Modern buildings, while addressing practical and economic needs, often disrupt the dialogue between past and present, risking the erasure of the subtle narratives embedded in older structures. The reflections offered in this chapter underscore the responsibility of architects, urban planners, and policymakers in shaping Istanbul's built environment. Designers today are challenged to balance innovation with sensitivity to historical context, ensuring that new constructions do not merely overwrite the city's memory but instead engage in a meaningful dialogue with it.

Ultimately, it conveys that Istanbul's identity is inseparable from its architecture, both old and new, and that every spatial transformation carries cultural, social, and emotional implications. It illuminates the ways in which architecture can preserve memory, evoke reflection, and sustain continuity across generations, while also highlighting the tensions introduced by modernization. By considering the perspectives of designers and the lived experiences of the city's inhabitants, the chapter positions Istanbul as a case study in the broader discourse of urban studies: a city where memory, identity, and architectural practice converge. This nuanced understanding reinforces the chapter's significance within the novel, illustrating that the preservation of architectural heritage, alongside thoughtful adaptation, is essential for maintaining the city's soul while negotiating the inevitable pressures of contemporary urban life.

By safeguarding these structures, urban planning may globally allow communities to retain a tangible connection with their heritage, fostering a sense of belonging and continuity.

At the same time, planning interventions also aim to accommodate contemporary needs, such as housing, transportation, and commercial spaces, ensuring that the city remains livable and functional. This dual approach demonstrates that heritage preservation and modern development need not be in opposition. Instead, thoughtful and carefully constructed urban planning can integrate old and new architecture, allowing historical buildings to coexist with contemporary designs in a way that respects both the city's memory and its evolving social fabric. The central argument of this chapter is to urge contemporary urban planners to approach the renovation of monumental sites with sensitivity, ensuring that infrastructural development such as road construction, large-scale infrastructural projects, transit corridors, public utilities does not erase the original architectural forms that embody generational memory. This study has made an endeavour to demonstrate how such an approach can be instrumentalized practically with the examples of few cities like Delhi, Kashmir, and Istanbul which have already actualized these patterns of reconstruction. The cases examined in this chapter, supported by pictorial documentation, seek to demonstrate how architectural and urban planning interventions can contribute to the restoration of memory in various forms, even if such restoration can never be fully recuperated. However, the limitation of this study lies in the impracticality of universally implementing this architectural approach; nevertheless, it advances the conviction and the hope that such constraints may be surmounted in the future.

Works Cited

- Ahmed, S., and N. Ahmad. *Architectural Heritage and Cultural Identity: The Case of Hagia Sophia. Journal of Cultural Heritage Studies*, 2022.
- Bayraktaroglu, S., and D. Öktem Erkartal. "Urban Memory and the Architecture of Continuity in Istanbul." *Journal of Urban History and Heritage*, vol. 8, no. 2, 2020, pp. 31–34.
- Bozdoğan, Sibel. *Modernism and Nation Building: Turkish Architectural Culture in the Early Republic.* University of Washington Press, 2001.
- Çelik, Zeynep. *The Remaking of Istanbul: Portrait of an Ottoman City in the Nineteenth Century.* University of California Press, 2004.
- Cormack, Robin. *Byzantine Art.* Oxford University Press, 2000.
- Cutler, A. "Structure and Aesthetic at Hagia Sophia in Constantinople." *Journal of the Society of Architectural Historians*, vol. 25, no. 4, 1966, pp. [tbd]. *JSTOR*.
- Durusoy Özmen, E. "Theodosian Walls and the

Continuity of Byzantine Urban Memory." *Byzantine Studies Review*, vol. 12, no. 3, 2019, pp. 582–583.
- Freely, John. *Istanbul: The Imperial City.* Penguin Books, 1998.
- Goodwin, Godfrey. *A History of Ottoman Architecture.* Thames and Hudson, 1971.
- Graham, Stephen, and Simon Marvin. *Splintering Urbanism: Networked Infrastructures, Technological Mobilities, and the Urban Condition.* Routledge, 2001.
- Gurses, Sevinç. "Hüzün and the Memory of Place in Orhan Pamuk's *Istanbul*." *Literature and Architecture Studies*, vol. 5, no. 3, 2010.
- Gupta, R. "Heritage and Urban Identity: Old Delhi's Architecture." *Indian Journal of Cultural Studies*, 2019, p. 45.
- "Hagia Sophia: Church, Mosque, Museum." *Oxford Research Encyclopaedia of Asian History*, 2024. Oxfordre.com.
- "Hagia Sophia: Through the Ages." *YouTube*, uploaded by [Uploader's Name], [upload date], www.youtube.com/watch?v=rqa0eXnDey4.
- Heller, Peter. "The Blue Mosque: Aesthetic Dialogue and Architectural Memory." *Architectural Review of the East*, 2022.
- Jabi, W. "Geometry, Light, and Cosmology in the Church of Hagia Sophia." *Proceedings of the IJAC Conference*, [date]. Papers.cumincad.org.
- Kaya, Ayşe. "Continuity and Transformation in Istanbul's Urban Heritage." *Middle Eastern Architectural Review*, 2020.
- Koul, S. "Modern Housing in Kashmir: Between

- Tradition and Transformation." *Kashmir Studies Quarterly*, 2018, p. 56.
- Krautheimer, Richard. *Early Christian and Byzantine Architecture*. Yale University Press, 1986.
- Kuban, Doğan. *Istanbul: An Urban History—Byzantion, Constantinopolis, Istanbul*. Türkiye İş Bankası Kültür Yayınları, 2010.
- Mainstone, Rowland J. *Hagia Sophia: Architecture, Structure, and Liturgy of Justinian's Great Church*. Thames and Hudson, 1988.
- Mango, Cyril A. *Byzantine Architecture*. Rizzoli, 1976.
- Mark, R., A. S. Cakmak, K. Hill, and R. Davidson. "Structural Analysis of Hagia Sophia: A Historical Perspective." *Soil Dynamics & Earthquake Engineering*, vol. 3, WIT Press / *Transactions on the Built Environment*, 1993.
- Mathews, Thomas F. *The Byzantine Churches of Istanbul: A Photographic Survey*. Pennsylvania State University Press, 1976.
- Necipoğlu, Gülru. *The Age of Sinan: Architectural Culture in the Ottoman Empire*. Reaktion Books, 2005.
- Nur, Yüksel Burçin, and F. Özer. "Hagia Sophia as a Palimpsest of Civilizations." *ICONARP International Journal of Architecture and Planning*, vol. 5, no. 2, 2017.
- Ousterhout, Robert. *Master Builders of Byzantium*. University of Pennsylvania Museum of Archaeology and Anthropology, 1999.
- Pamuk, Orhan. *Istanbul: Memories and the City*. Translated by Maureen Freely, Knopf, 2005.
- Pandit, R. "Traditional Kashmiri Architecture:

Sustainability and Identity." *South Asian Architecture Journal*, 2017, p. 102.
- Şahin, O. Erdal. "The Construction of Hagia Sophia as an Imperial Space and the Process of Change." *Balkan and Near Eastern Journal of Social Sciences*, vol. 5, no. 3, 2019–2020.
- Sev, Ayla, and M. Başarır. "Byzantine Influence on Ottoman Architectural Space." *Anatolian Architecture Journal*, vol. 4, 2018, pp. 22–23.
- Sharma, V. "Colonial Urban Planning in Lutyens' Delhi." *Urban Studies of India*, 2016, p. 78.
- UNESCO. *Topkapi Palace: World Heritage Site Report.* UNESCO World Heritage Centre, 2019.
- Volait, Mercedes, and Nazan Avcıoğlu. *Architectural Crossings: Byzantium and the Ottoman World.* Routledge, 2019, pp. 112–118.

Chapter – 4

The Spatialization of Trauma: Sites of Violence and Forgetting

How Do Spaces Remember Violence

This chapter interrogates the dialectics of remembering and forgetting as they manifest across global geographies of trauma. It asks how spaces remember violence and whether architecture and urban planning possess the capacity to heal or conversely perpetuate collective trauma. Through a critical engagement with sites such as Ground Zero in New York, Hiroshima's Genbaku Dome, Jallianwala Bagh in Amritsar, Bhubaneswar and Puri of Odisha, the siege-scarred streets of Sarajevo, the Kigali Genocide Memorial, and Berlin's Holocaust Memorial, the discussion illuminates how urban landscapes perform as archives of suffering. These spaces, shaped by distinct historical contingencies yet united by a shared phenomenology of loss, foreground the uneasy relationship between aesthetic form and ethical remembrance.

In mapping trauma onto space, this chapter seeks to unravel the politics of visibility that govern memorial design and spatial reconstruction. It proposes that the architectural encoding of violence is never neutral: it mediates between the moral imperative to remember and the sociopolitical desire to forget. The spatialization of trauma, therefore, is not only a matter of design but of conscience a negotiation between the persistence of the past and the architectures of the present that seek to contain it.

Within the discourse of contemporary memory studies, the critical focus has shifted decisively from the textual to the spatial, from narrating trauma through language to reading it through the grammar of place and space. Pierre Nora's concept of *lieux de mémoire* marked a pivotal reorientation in this discourse, positing sites of memory as cultural constructs that emerge when the continuity of lived memory is disrupted (Nora 7). Andreas Huyssen further expanded this spatial turn, contending that modern cities operate as "palimpsests of memory," where the simultaneity of past and present produces both mnemonic density and historical amnesia (*Present Pasts* 25). Likewise, Aleida Assmann underscores the dynamic interplay between *storage memory* (the archival) and *functional memory* (the performative), suggesting that spatial practices, monuments, ruins, and memorial architectures mediate this tension by externalizing collective remembrance into tangible form (*Cultural Memory and Western Civilization* 98).

Topographies of Ruin: Spatial Memories of Violence and Forgetting:

Ruins of architecture may be understood as sediments of violence and physical sites where histories of atrocity, conflict and repression persist in the material substratum of place. What appears as broken masonry or scarred façades is often a complex inscription of trauma, memory, and forgetting. As urban scholar Andreas Huyssen argues, the modern city is "a palimpsest of memory" where the past and present co-exist in charged relation (Huyssen 25). In parallel, Aleida Assmann reminds us that memory must be understood both as an archival deposit and as a performative, spatial practice (Assmann 98). More recently, Avishek Parui's work on "mnemonic mobility" and the materiality of memory in the postcolonial South Asian context gives new purchase to thinking about how violence becomes encoded into space (Parui 2022).

This chapter interrogates how architecture and urban design become repositories of violence and how they function not simply as memorials but as contested fields of memory, forgetting, and commodification. It argues How do ruins of violence mediate memory through space? And further: Do they offer a possibility of ethical reckoning or slip into commodification and erasure? Through close examination of four global sites i.e. the Hiroshima Peace Memorial (Genbaku Dome), Jallianwala Bagh in Amritsar, Topography of Terror in Berlin, and Sniper Alley in Sarajevo this chapter explores how ruins operate as spatial testimonies of violence and how their aestheticization can oscillate between remembrance and commodification.

The concept of architectural ruin has long served as a metaphor for decline, loss, and historicity. Yet, when tied to the memory of violence, ruins also become *witness buildings* fragments that testify to irrecoverable loss. Henri Lefebvre's *production of space* (1991: 38) reminds us that built space is socially and politically produced; thus, ruins of violence may be read as the leftover logics of power and conflict. Parui's notion of "material-mnemonics" emphasises how objects, architecture and space mediate violence and memory in tandem (Parui 2022).

Ruins, then, perform dual functions. On one hand, they signal rupture and bear the scars of some violent event, an interruption in time. On the other, they invite reinterpretation as they become sites of commemoration, tourism, national narrative or even spectacle. The tension between these two poles between *memory* and *forgetting* is central. As Paul Ricoeur writes, memory always bears within it the possibility of forgetting; the two are dialectically bound (Ricoeur 2004: 89). In the built environment, the aesthetic of ruin can catalyse reflection and mourning; or it can be harnessed for spectacle, consumption and commodification.

Hiroshima Peace Memorial (Genbaku Dome)

The Hiroshima Peace Memorial, known as the Genbaku Dome, remains the skeletal ruin of the industrial promotion hall that survived the atomic bomb of 6 August 1945. Its official UNESCO description states that the preserved structure serves as "a stark and powerful symbol of the most destructive force ever created by humankind" (UNESCO 1996). The building has been kept in its immediate post-explosion state, its walls fractured, its steel supports exposed, its form skeletal but preserved. This act of preservation is itself an architectural gesture of witness: the ruin is not restored to pristine condition but maintained as an active sign of violence.

The site thus operates as a moral and spatial injunction: to remember but also to work for peace. However, even here the aesthetic of ruin raises questions. The dome sits within a constructed Peace Memorial Park a landscaped, curated environment. The risk is that the ruin becomes a picturesque object rather than a site of ethical engagement. The question arises: does the architectural preservation of the dome genuinely assist collective trauma-work, or does it permit a commodified, globalised form of memory tourism?

Jallianwala Bagh, Amritsar

In the narrow walled garden of Jallianwala Bagh in Punjab, the massacre of 13 April 1919 remains physically legible: bullet-scarred walls, the well into which the crowds jumped to escape bullets, and the narrow entryway through which British troops blocked exit (Amritsar Tourism 2025). The site thus embodies violence in the urban fabric. The garden's transformation into a memorial site in 1961 and its recent redevelopment have elicited critique: some commentators argue that newer galleries, murals and landscaping risk "Disneyfication" of atrocity (Indian Express 2021). Here the aesthetics of ruin (bullet holes, narrow lane, Martyr's Well) jostle with modern memorial architecture and tourist infrastructure.

The site illustrates how ruins of colonial violence may be re-inscribed within national narratives of freedom and identity. The retention of open wounds (the well, the bullet marks) confers authenticity, but the subsequent memorial architecture can shift focus from the embodied trauma to its spectacle. Here we witness the dual movement of memory and forgetting: the architecture conveys memory, but the commercialisation and sanitisation of the space risk forgetting.

Berlin's Topography of Terror

Located on the former site of the Gestapo and SS headquarters in Nazi Germany, the Topography of Terror in Berlin is a deliberately curated ruin-museum. In situ architectural fragments (sections of the Berlin Wall, foundations) are combined with a modern museum structure and outdoor displays. The ruin is leveraged as moral pedagogy: the architecture itself becomes a didactic tool, calling attention to state-sponsored violence and the complicity of bureaucratic modernity.

The architecture of ruin here is sophisticated: it is not a nostalgic ruin but a curated one. It uses discontinuity, voids, exposed foundations to provoke reflection. Yet, as critic Karen Till suggests, the very act of turning ruin into tourist monument can risk "heritage spectacle" (Till 2005: 13). The architecture may heal by fostering ethical witnessing; but it may also perpetuate forgetting by sanitising violence into museum aesthetics.

Sniper Alley, Sarajevo

During the 1992-95 siege of Sarajevo, certain boulevards became known as "Sniper Alley" where civilians were shot by snipers from high rises. Post-conflict urban renewal has seen the removal or renovation of many of these façades. What remains often are ghost-buildings, bullet-scarred façades, invasive netting, or memorial plaques. The urban fabric thus continues to bear trauma.

Here, the ruin is not monumentalised as a singular memorial building but dispersed across the cityscape an everyday ruin that lives in residences, façades and public realm. This raises different architectural questions: How does ordinary urban fabric serve as a palimpsest of violence? Has the city's renewal erased too much? In Sarajevo, the tension lies between rebuilding for normalcy and preserving the scars of war as memory carriers. The danger of forgetting becomes vivid when facades are cleaned, high-rise developments replace emptied lots, and international aid glosses over embedded trauma.

Between Remembrance and Commodification

Across these sites, three interrelated dynamics of ruin-memory emerge:

1. **Aestheticisation of Violence**: Ruins become objects of visual consumption. The Genbaku Dome and Topography of Terror attract international visitors, but this very attention can trivialise trauma through tourism. As Parui argues, memory becomes *mobilised* when it is rendered into material form and circulated raising risks of commodification (Parui 2022).
2. **Selective Visibility and Erasure**: What is kept visible (bullet holes, ruins) and what is erased (surrounding context, civilian narratives) is a political decision. Jallianwala Bagh's redevelopment has been criticised for erasing the "rawness" of the massacre site. In Sarajevo, many trauma-scapes have been overwritten by "normal" urban development.
3. **Temporal Suspension**: Ruins often freeze a moment of violence in time, yet good memorial architecture acknowledges the flow of time, including the ongoing nature of trauma. When architecture treats violence as past and closed, it risks closure rather than engagement. Parui uses the term "mnemonic

mobility" to emphasise memory that moves across time, not that which is frozen (Parui 2022).

Thus, the architecture of ruin is ambiguous: it can facilitate ethical witnessing, a form of spatial justice, but also participate in forgetting—either by sanitising, commodifying or aesthetically neutralising violence.

The Politics of Forgetting: Erasure, Gentrification, and Selective Memory

In the neoliberal reconfiguration of global cities, forgetting emerges not merely as an absence of memory but as a politically orchestrated act of spatial and cultural erasure. Modern redevelopment regimes steeped in the aesthetics of progress and marketability systematically overwrite the mnemonic textures of urban space. As Andreas Huyssen (2003) observes in *Present Pasts*, contemporary urbanism is marked by a paradoxical simultaneity: an obsession with memory coexisting with rampant forms of forgetting. Within this dialectic, cities become archives of selective remembrance, where trauma, displacement, and dissent are sanitized to accommodate global capital and the aesthetic economies of modernity. Gentrification, urban renewal, and heritage branding act as mechanisms through which cities commodify nostalgia while erasing histories of violence, resistance, and marginality. The politics of forgetting thus operates spatially through architectural amnesia, material displacement, and representational control.

Urban Amnesia in India and Odisha: The Erasures of Development

In India's rapidly transforming urban topography,

architectural amnesia manifests through the logic of redevelopment and gentrification. Old Delhi, Bhubaneswar, and Mumbai illustrate how neoliberal aspirations systematically overwrite historical textures.

In Bhubaneswar, the planned capital of Odisha designed by Otto Königsberger in the 1940s, modernist planning coexisted uneasily with the region's ancient architectural heritage. The juxtaposition of the Lingaraj Temple complex and the postcolonial grid-like city reflects a *spatial palimpsest* a living negotiation between memory and modernization. Yet, recent real estate expansion and "Smart City" initiatives have threatened to efface indigenous architectural traditions and vernacular urbanism. What emerges, as Vandana Baweja (2010) notes, is a form of *developmental forgetting*, where progress demands erasure of older urban morphologies.

Similarly, the restructuring of Puri's sacred geography under the Smart City Mission has displaced hundreds of residents in the name of pilgrimage infrastructure. These erasures are not merely physical but ontological; they fracture the city's lived memory. As Ashis Nandy (2001) reminds us, "modernity's violence often comes not through the gun but through the bulldozer," manifesting as cultural and mnemonic violence. When Otto Königsberger designed Bhubaneswar as the new capital of Odisha in 1948, his modernist grid aimed to symbolize a rational, secular future in contrast to the sacred and labyrinthine cityscapes of Old Town. Yet this planning process, as K.C. Mallick (2015) observes, enacted a subtle displacement of indigenous spatial logic, the organic coexistence of ritual pathways (*yātras*), temple clusters, and community courtyards that had historically defined Odisha's urban life.

The modernist design, modeled on Le Corbusier's Chandigarh, imposed a geometry of control, dividing sacred and administrative zones and institutionalizing memory into the museum rather than the street. The State Museum and Khandagiri-Udayagiri sites were reconstituted as heritage enclaves, while living practices around the Lingaraj Temple precinct were increasingly marginalized. This represents what David Harvey (1989) calls *"spatial disciplining"* the use of architecture to enforce ideological order. The "Smart City" rejuvenation of Bhubaneswar further amplifies this logic: in its attempt to brand the city as "livable and global," it privileges technology over tradition, aesthetics over ancestry, and visibility over vernacular intimacy.

Thus, Bhubaneswar's story is not merely about progress but about the silent erasure of mnemonic geographies, where the memory of older settlements and craft clusters is overwritten by steel, glass, and concrete.

Puri: Sacred Geography and the Violence of Beautification

The recent Heritage Corridor Project around the Jagannath Temple in Puri offers a striking example of how sacred memory is being reconfigured under the guise of development. The project, which involves clearing residential zones and centuries-old *mutts* (monastic houses) within a 75-meter radius of the temple, has led to the displacement of families and ritual practitioners whose daily lives form the living archive of Puri's religious culture.

As Das (2022) points out, this process constitutes

a form of mnemonic violence, where architectural heritage is reduced to monumental aesthetics, severed from its performative and communal dimensions. The corridors and plazas being constructed seek to create a "world-class pilgrim experience," yet in doing so, they erase the intricate spatial intimacy between deity, devotee, and dwellings that defined the *kshetra*.

This act of *beautification as obliteration* aligns with Sharon Macdonald's (2009) notion of "heritage sanitization," where development selectively preserves structures while silencing the messy, embodied practices that gave them meaning. The displacement of *sevayats* (temple servants) and local residents, many of whom trace lineage to medieval religious orders, underscores how modern state projects rewrite sacred space as spectacle, converting lived memory into architectural branding.

Cuttack: The Forgotten City of Memory

Cuttack, once the capital of Odisha and one of the oldest continuously inhabited cities in Eastern India, presents another dimension of urban forgetting. The city's colonial and precolonial legacies, including its Barabati Fort, Mahanadi riverfront, and dense neighborhood networks are steadily vanishing under infrastructural neglect and uneven development. As S. Mishra (2018) notes, Cuttack embodies "a history without a monument," where the absence of state investment translates into the slow decay of cultural memory.

Gentrification in the form of unplanned commercial growth has overwhelmed the city's distinctive moorings, its Maratha-era temples, Bengali settlements, and riverine trading ghats, creating what could be termed a *vernacular ruinology*. The city survives as a lived archive, yet without institutional frameworks of preservation, its mnemonic landscape dissolves into anonymity. Cuttack thus stands as a counterpoint to Bhubaneswar's over-curated memory where oblivion results not from overdevelopment but from neglect, a different face of forgetting within postcolonial modernity.

Industrial and Coastal Displacements:
The Vanishing Memory of Place

Beyond the urban core, Odisha's industrial expansion particularly in Paradeep, Kalinganagar, and Jharsuguda has generated a different form of spatial erasure. Large-scale industrial corridors, port projects, and mining operations have displaced indigenous and rural communities, fragmenting traditional spatial consciousness.

In Kalinganagar (2006), the violent suppression of tribal resistance to land acquisition by corporate conglomerates exemplified the biopolitical cost of development. The erasure here is both physical and epistemic: the landscape's mnemonic density ritual sites, ancestral groves, burial grounds has been flattened into industrial geography. As Nandini Sundar (2016) argues, such displacements signify "the obliteration of memory as resource," where modernization destroys the very ecological and cultural matrices that sustain community identity.

Similarly, the post-2019 Cyclone Fani reconstruction along Odisha's coastal belt has resulted in the development of planned "resilient townships." While these initiatives are guided by the principles of climate-conscious urban planning, they often lead to the erasure of older vernacular coastal settlements. The memory of disaster is thus absorbed into the rhetoric of resilience, transforming trauma into a developmental narrative, a hallmark of what Andreas Huyssen (2003) calls "the politics of temporal compression."

Mnemonic Fragmentation and the Postcolonial Present

Across these examples from Odisha, Bhubaneswar's planned amnesia, Puri's sacred displacements, Cuttack's neglect, and Kalinganagar's industrial erasure the underlying process is the same: selective remembrance. The state and market curate what is to be preserved (temples, facades, corridors) and what is to be forgotten (rituals, residents, histories). This selective curation transforms the city into an archive without affect, what Ariella Azoulay (2019) calls "an archive of imperial dispositions" constructed to serve visibility but not memory. Odisha's case thereby reveals the scalar dynamics of forgetting: how the local folds into the national and global, how the politics of space manifests as a politics of memory. Paradoxically enough, It highlights the postcolonial paradox wherein remembrance and erasure coexist and developmental projects commemorate progress even as they obliterate the very past that enabled it.

After apartheid, the establishment of the District Six Museum in 1994 sought to recuperate this erased history. Yet, the museum itself exists within an ambivalent memory economy. Its important to note here that it memorializes absent photographs of vanished streets, fragments of personal belongings, and hand-drawn maps, but is also integrated into a heritage industry that commodifies trauma for cultural tourism. Steven Robins and Annie Coombes both note how such heritage sites walk a fine line between counter-memory and neoliberal spectacle, turning sites of resistance into curated zones of reconciliation.

Thus, District Six demonstrates the contradiction of post-apartheid urban memory: while the rhetoric of restitution acknowledges historical injustice, the physical return of land and the reconstruction of space remain largely unrealized. The void of District Six partly rebuilt, partly preserved in ruins symbolizes a spatial melancholia, where the desire to remember coexists with the impossibility of full restoration.

2. Nanjing Massacre Memorial Hall: Monumentality and the Politics of National Memory

The Nanjing Massacre Memorial Hall, built in 1985 and expanded in 2007, represents another form of selective memorialization this time at the intersection of trauma, nationalism, and state-controlled remembrance. The massacre, committed by the Japanese Imperial Army in 1937, claimed over 300,000 Chinese lives. Yet, the process of remembering this atrocity is shaped by what Kirk Denton (2014) calls "the politics of display" the negotiation between mourning and nation-building.

In the late 20th century, China's shift from revolutionary communism to neoliberal nationalism reoriented memory politics. The memorial hall, designed by Qi Kang, employs stark, brutalist architecture: rough concrete textures, mass graves, and mournful sculptures, producing a visceral encounter with loss. However, the site's aesthetic and narrative choices reveal a highly curated mnemonic order. The memorial monumentalizes suffering not as open trauma but as a pedagogical tool of patriotism, aligning collective grief with the rhetoric of national resurgence.

Pierre Nora's notion of *lieux de mémoire* (1989) helps interpret this transformation: the memorial hall functions as a "site of memory" precisely because real social memory has dissipated. As China urbanized rapidly under neoliberal modernity, the physical memorial became a substitute for lived remembrance. In this sense, the memorial's spatial aesthetics the monumental voids, the ritualized exhibits perform aesthetic containment of trauma.

Moreover, the museum's expansion into a global tourist site has layered commercial memory practices atop its original commemorative intent. As Carol Gluck (2007) suggests, global memory circuits often turn sites of atrocity into "mnemonic capital", generating affective and economic value simultaneously. Thus, the Nanjing Memorial participates in a form of memory gentrification—the transformation of suffering into state-managed spectacle, where the politics of forgetting resides not in neglect, but in strategic remembrance that neutralizes dissent.

3. Partition Sites in India and Pakistan: Absence, Silence, and the Architecture of Amnesia

Unlike the overt memorialization of Nanjing or District Six, the Partition of India and Pakistan (1947) remain one of the least memorialized cataclysms of the 20th century, despite its staggering scale of displacement and death. Over 14 million people were uprooted, and an estimated one million perished. Yet, the urban landscapes of

Delhi, Lahore, Amritsar, and Karachi bear no monumental acknowledgment of this shared trauma. The absence itself becomes a mnemonic structure, an architecture of forgetting.

Urvashi Butalia (1998) and Gyanendra Pandey (2001) have argued that Partition's silences are political: both postcolonial states constructed nationhood through selective amnesia, suppressing narratives that complicated their foundational myths. Remembering Partition would mean confronting the violence of origin the "intimate enemy" within, as Ashis Nandy puts it. Consequently, cities that once embodied shared cultural memory became zones of erasure. Muslim homes in Delhi, abandoned Hindu temples in Lahore, and renamed streets across Punjab constitute what Michel de Certeau (1984) calls "ghostly topographies" of urban traces that resist the state's attempt to impose coherence.

Architecturally, this amnesia manifests in urban repurposing. Refugee camps became permanent colonies; damaged havelis were demolished; border towns were modernized into bureaucratic spaces of surveillance. The physical and affective geographies of Partition were thus overwritten by the developmentalist language of modernity. As Vazira Zamindar (2007) notes, the refugee body was assimilated into the nation-building narrative, while the memory of displacement was absorbed into the rhetoric of progress.

This silence contrasts sharply with the later emergence of grassroots memory initiatives digital archives, oral history projects, and temporary exhibitions that attempt to re-inscribe Partition memory into the public sphere.

Yet, these efforts remain fragmented and largely marginal to urban planning discourses. The absence of official memorials underscores the state's investment in forgetting, where amnesia operates as an instrument of cohesion in the fragile postcolonial polity.

4. Architectural Amnesia and the Global Aesthetic of Erasure

Across these cases, a common pattern emerges: the city becomes a palimpsest of forgetting, where erasure itself produces meaning. As Andreas Huyssen (2003) observes, "the urban imaginary thrives on the tension between the desire to remember and the compulsion to forget." In each context Cape Town, Nanjing and Delhi, the politics of memory unfold through architecture: what is built, what is demolished, and what remains in ruin.

Neoliberal redevelopment often disguises itself as aesthetic renewal, yet it performs a deeper mnemonic violence. District Six's emptiness, Nanjing's monumentalization, and Partition's silence all reveal distinct strategies of managing the past. The neoliberal and postcolonial city thus becomes an archive of absences, where selective memory legitimizes authority while displacing marginal histories.

This processes what Sharon Macdonald (2013) terms *"heritage from below"* turned *"heritage for consumption"* transforms urban memory into a marketable resource. The politics of forgetting is therefore not merely an epistemic condition but a spatial practice enacted in stone, skyline, and street name through which the modern city continuously rewrites its own narrative.

Architecture as Catharsis : The Aesthetics of Remembering

The question of how architecture mediates collective trauma has become central to contemporary debates on memory and urban ethics. Architecture, as both material construct and symbolic language, performs the dual role of mourning and myth-making. It oscillates between two competing impulses one therapeutic, the other theatrical manifesting what Andreas Huyssen calls the "urban palimpsest," where the past persists as trace and affect within the city's surfaces (Huyssen 2003). The dialectic of *architecture as catharsis* versus *architecture as spectacle* thus frames the politics of memory: whether architecture heals through remembrance or dazzles through representation.

Architecture as Catharsis

Architecture as catharsis arises from the Aristotelian notion of *katharsis* /Catharsis, the purgation of emotions through structured aesthetic experience. In memorial design, this translates into spaces that invite introspection, silence, and ethical confrontation with history. James E. Young's theory of the *counter-monument* argues that the most meaningful memorials are those that refuse closure, compelling ongoing dialogue rather than offering emotional resolution (*The Texture of Memory*, 1993). Daniel Libeskind's *Jewish Museum* in Berlin exemplifies this ethos: its fractured corridors, voids, and dead ends materialize the impossibility of narrative completion. The building itself becomes a vessel of absence a spatial metaphor for loss that refuses reconciliation.

Similarly, in the Indian context, the *Jallianwala Bagh Memorial* at Amritsar enacts catharsis through the raw endurance of the site. The preserved bullet holes on the walls and the narrow entrance evoke the embodied terror of colonial violence. Here, architecture acts as a mnemonic wound, maintaining the visceral presence of trauma without succumbing to aesthetic comfort. These spaces operate as affective archives — not as perfected art objects, but as ethical provocations that resist forgetting.

In Odisha, the neglected yet potent *Kalinga War site* near Dhauli embodies an alternate cathartic mode. While Ashoka's edicts proclaim remorse and transformation, the modern monument built nearby reduces that memory to monumental symbolism. The tension between the textual and the architectural reflects how catharsis can be undermined when political narratives overdetermine the affective potential of space.

Architecture as Spectacle

Conversely, the spectacularization of trauma converts memory into consumable experience. In an era dominated by neoliberal urbanism, the memorial landscape often aligns with what Guy Debord termed the *society of the spectacle* (Debord 1967). Here, memory becomes commodified — embedded within tourism, nation-branding, and aesthetic display. The "performative mourning" that Judith Butler critiques in *Precarious Life* (2004) applies aptly: grief, when publicly orchestrated, risks becoming spectacle rather than solidarity.

This dynamic is evident in the transformation of Ground Zero in New York into a sanitized memorial park complex. The architectural language of the *National September 11 Memorial* blends sacred minimalism with monumental affect, yet its surrounding commercial redevelopment, the One World Trade Center, dilutes the site's memorial gravity. The memory of loss merges with the logic of capitalism and consumption. As Slavoj Žižek provocatively notes, such memorial spectacles often *repress* the reality of trauma by over-representing it as a catharsis that becomes anaesthetic rather than ethical.

In Asia, the *Nanjing Massacre Memorial Hall* exemplifies both the power and peril of monumental mourning. The brutal aesthetic thus projects the solemnity of national trauma, yet its curatorial strategies often serve state narratives of victimhood and redemption. The memorial, therefore, becomes an instrument of political legitimation, aestheticizing trauma through monumental affect while suppressing plural memory. Similarly, the *Partition Museum* in Amritsar curates collective grief through immersive installations, yet its spatial cartography risks transforming suffering into spectacle, a carefully staged "affective tourism" (Sarkar 2020).

Performative Mourning and the Aestheticization of Trauma

The tension between catharsis and spectacle crystallizes in the phenomenon of performative mourning, where grief is enacted through ritualized, aesthetic, or media-mediated gestures rather than lived ethical engagement. Jacques Rancière's notion of the "distribution of the sensible" (2004) is crucial here as to Ranciere, the politics of mourning depends on what can be seen, heard, and represented. In this sense, architecture becomes a stage upon which states, institutions, and publics perform their allegiance to memory while simultaneously controlling its visual and emotional registers.

This aestheticization of trauma is not merely formal, rather it is ideological. As Sharon Macdonald argues in *Memorylands* (2013), heritage industries often replace historical complexity with "consumable memoryscapes."(Macdonald 33) The memorial becomes an object of aesthetic pleasure, a beautiful ruin rather than a site of ethical reckoning. In cities like Bhubaneswar, "smart city" projects that reconstruct heritage corridors (such as those around the Lingaraj Temple) exemplify this process. Traditional neighborhoods are cleared in the name of heritage preservation, producing what Nandini Sundar calls "spatial cleansing," an urban memory sanitized for tourist gaze and global capital.

Toward an Ethics of Remembrance

To navigate between catharsis and spectacle, an ethics of remembrance must guide memorial architecture. This entails designing spaces that provoke discomfort rather than closure, dialogic engagement rather than passive reverence. As Libeskind insists, "architecture must become the site of memory itself, not its representation." In practice, this could mean maintaining ruins, scars, and absences as active spatial testimonies. Such an approach transforms architecture into a medium of witnessing rather than a spectacle of redemption.

In Odisha and other postcolonial spaces, where trauma is often unacknowledged from displacement due to development, and the erasure of tribal lands is not to monumentalize grief but to spatialize resistance. The politics of forgetting can only be countered by architectures of testimony spaces that refuse amnesia through presence, trace, and vulnerability.

Visual Essays: Cartographies of Trauma (Memorial Landscapes and archival photos)

Khan, Shahid Ahmad, ImageID153704326.:https://www.dreamstime.com

Khan, Shahid Ahmad. Old Kashmiri Traditional Wooden House, Srinagar, Jammu and Kashmir, India. Dreamstime,ImageID153704326.URL:https://www.dreamstime.com/old-kashmiri-traditional-wooden-house-srinagar-jammu-kashmir-india-image153704326, The photograph titled *Old Kashmiri Traditional Wooden House, Srinagar, Jammu and Kashmir, India* by Shahid Ahmad Khan (Dreamstime, Image ID 153704326) captures the architectural soul of Kashmir with remarkable ethnographic precision. This structure exemplifies the synthesis of indigenous craftsmanship and climatic intelligence that defines the region's vernacular architecture. Built primarily from locally sourced timber and stone, the house demonstrates how materiality becomes memory; each carved lattice, wooden bracket, and projecting bay window (known locally as *daji devar*) reflects centuries of adaptation to cold climates and seismic conditions. Khan's image functions as more than architectural documentation; it operates as a visual narrative of cultural endurance. The interlacing of wood and stone symbolizes the coexistence of fragility and strength, an aesthetic metaphor for Kashmiri identity itself, shaped by history, conflict, and resilience. The structure's tiered elevations and enclosed balconies create both privacy and openness, echoing the region's social fabric, where interior life unfolds inwardly yet remains deeply connected to the natural surroundings.

Memory and Topography: Orhan Pamuk and the Urban Space | 163

Heritage House in Srinagar, Jammu and Kashmir.
Photograph. Accessed 2 Nov. 2025.

Heritage House in Srinagar, Jammu and Kashmir. Photograph. Accessed 2 Nov. 2025. The photograph titled *Heritage House in Srinagar, Jammu and Kashmir* captures the grandeur and layered history of traditional Kashmiri domestic architecture. Though the photographer remains unnamed, the image itself functions as a cultural document, preserving the architectural vocabulary of a region where every beam, balcony, and carved window narrates the story of time. The house exemplifies the vernacular sophistication of Srinagar's heritage structures, multi-tiered facades built with a rhythmic interplay of brick, timber, and intricately carved walnut wood. The projecting *jharokhas* (balconies) and arched fenestrations display of an architectural grammar shaped by both Mughal aesthetics and local craftsmanship, revealing how regional identity finds expression through modern structure and ornament.

Traditional Haveli Entrance, Old Delhi, India. Photograph. uploaded by City Heritage India, 2023.

Traditional Haveli Entrance, Old Delhi, India. Photograph. uploaded by City Heritage India, 2023. The photograph titled *Traditional Haveli Entrance, Old Delhi, India* (Unsplash, uploaded by City Heritage India, 2023) encapsulates the architectural intimacy and ornamental depth which is a chief characteristic of Mughal-era domestic architecture in North India. The haveli's entrance, framed by intricately carved arches and recessed niches, reveals how craftsmanship functioned as both aesthetic expression and social identity. Each carved surface, floral motif, and geometrical detail articulates a language of hospitality and hierarchy, marking the transition between public street and private home, a threshold space where cultural rituals of entry and belonging unfold.

Beards, Dr. Graham. *Bullet-marked Wall at Jallianwala Bagh, Amritsar, India*. 2 Nov. 2025 Wikimedia Commons, https://commons.wikimedia.org/wiki/File:Jallianwala_Bagh_Bullet_Marked_Wall.JPG.

The *Jallianwala Bagh Memorial* in Amritsar stands as a spatial manifestation of collective trauma, a site where history and psychology converge through architectural silence (*Jallianwala Bagh Memorial, Amritsar, Punjab, India*). The weathered red-brick walls, still bearing bullet scars, act as psychic imprints of violence, transforming the structure into a living archive of pain. Rather than reconstructing loss, the memorial preserves it, allowing absence to speak louder than form. Its narrow passages and enclosed geometry evoke the fear and confinement of that fateful day in 1919, translating historical brutality into spatial experience. Architecturally, it reflects a philosophy of restraint and remembrance. The minimal intervention honors authenticity, enabling the visitor's body to remember what the mind cannot fully articulate. From a psychological lens, the site becomes a ritual of witnessing, where every step reenacts the nation's suppressed grief.

Aerial View of the Jagannath Temple Heritage Corridor Project, Puri." NDTV, 17 Jan. 2024, www.ndtv.com/india-news/naveen-patnaik-inaugurates-rs-800-crore-heritage-corridor-at-puris-jagannath-temple-4880253.

Hiroshima Peace Memorial (Genbaku Dome), Hiroshima, Japan. Photograph by Fg2, 2007. *Wikimedia Commons*, https://commons.wikimedia.org/wiki/File:Genbaku_Dome04-r.JPG. Accessed 2 Nov. 2025

Works Cited

- Appadurai, Arjun. *Modernity at Large: Cultural Dimensions of Globalization*. University of Minnesota Press, 1996.
- Azoulay, Ariella Aïsha. *Potential History: Unlearning Imperialism*. Verso, 2019.
- Baweja, Vandana. "Otto Koenigsberger and the Planning of Bhubaneswar: The Architecture of a New Capital for a Newly Independent Nation." *Journal of the Society of Architectural Historians*, vol. 69, no. 2, 2010, pp. 149–171.
- Butalia, Urvashi. *The Other Side of Silence: Voices from the Partition of India*. Penguin Books, 1998.
- Das, Debojyoti. "Pilgrimage, Heritage, and Displacement: Politics of Temple Corridors in Puri." *Economic and Political Weekly*, vol. 57, no. 43, 2022, pp. 52–60.
- Foucault, Michel. "Of Other Spaces." *Diacritics*, vol. 16, no. 1, 1986, pp. 22–27.
- Gluck, Carol. "Operations of Memory: 'Comfort Women' and the World." In Sheila Miyoshi Jager and Rana Mitter (eds.), *Ruptured Histories: War, Memory, and the Post–Cold War in Asia*. Harvard University Press, 2007, pp. 47–77.
- Harvey, David. *The Condition of Postmodernity: An Enquiry into the Origins of Cultural Change*. Blackwell, 1989.
- Harvey, David. *Spaces of Hope*. University of California Press, 2000.
- Huyssen, Andreas. *Present Pasts: Urban Palimpsests and the Politics of Memory*. Stanford University Press, 2003.

- Macdonald, Sharon. *Memorylands: Heritage and Identity in Europe Today*. Routledge, 2013.
- Mallick, K. C. "Urban Planning and Cultural Continuity: The Case of Bhubaneswar." *Indian Journal of Urban Studies*, vol. 12, no. 1, 2015, pp. 22–39.
- Mishra, S. "Cuttack: A City of Memory and Forgetting." *Odisha Review*, vol. 74, no. 4, 2018, pp. 34–41.
- Nandy, Ashis. *An Ambiguous Journey to the City: The Village and Other Odd Ruins of the Self in the Indian Imagination*. Oxford University Press, 2001.
- Nora, Pierre. "Between Memory and History: Les Lieux de Mémoire." *Representations*, no. 26, 1989, pp. 7–24.
- Pandey, Gyanendra. *Remembering Partition: Violence, Nationalism and History in India*. Cambridge University Press, 2001.
- Robins, Steven. *From Revolution to Rights in South Africa: Social Movements, NGOs and Popular Politics after Apartheid*. University of KwaZulu-Natal Press, 2008.
- Sundar, Nandini. *The Burning Forest: India's War in Bastar*. Juggernaut, 2016.
- Young, James E. *The Texture of Memory: Holocaust Memorials and Meaning*. Yale University Press, 1993.

Chapter-5

Conclusion

Towards a Memory-Based Urban Consciousness

This book concludes by affirming that the future of urban design must be guided by a deep ethical awareness of memory as both method and material. Drawing upon the theoretical foundations of Henri Lefebvre's spatial triad where conceived, perceived, and lived spaces intersect and inspired by Orhan Pamuk's evocative cartography of remembrance, the study underscores that cities are not merely infrastructural assemblages but mnemonic ecologies shaped by affect, loss, and belonging. Within this framework, memory-sensitive urbanism emerges as both a critique and a proposition: a critique of developmental paradigms that pursue uniformity through erasure, and a proposition for an urban future grounded in the preservation of emotional and cultural topography.

      Pamuk's Istanbul, as examined throughout this study, dismantles the illusion of spatial homogeneity. His memoir renders the city as a palimpsest of emotions, where decay, nostalgia, and renewal coexist in an intricate cartography of remembrance. In doing so, this study challenges the Cartesian logic of state-controlled urban planning what Lefebvre would term space le conçu by privileging the lived, affective, and subjective dimensions of urban experience. This mode of remembering through narrative offers an epistemological model for architects and planners, to think of space as performed and remembered, rather than merely designed and executed.

The comparative explorations in the previous chapter shows how Mumbai's Dadabhai Naoroji Road, Jodhpur's Birkha Bawari Stepwell, and Seoul's Seoullo 7017 reaffirm that memory need not obstruct modernization; it can, instead, animate continuity. These cases illuminate how adaptive reuse and participatory planning can reconcile technological innovation with mnemonic depth. In each instance, architecture operates as a temporal bridge linking the symbolic and the functional, the emotional and the material. This aligns with Aldo Rossi's idea of the *urban artifact* as a repository of collective memory (*The Architecture of the City*), and extends to Jan Assmann's notion of *cultural memory* as an active medium of historical consciousness.

Thus, the central argument of this work insists that preservation is not nostalgia rather it is resistance to amnesia. Urban erasures carried out in the name of progress often perpetuate ideological silencing, privileging a monolithic narrative of the nation over the multiplicity of lived histories. By contrast, memory-sensitive planning envisions a plural, dialogic city that respects its sedimented histories while remaining open to change. It redefines progress not as the replacement of the old with the new, but as the capacity to

integrate continuity within transformation.

In this light, architectural conservation and urban design acquire a moral dimension. The city becomes an ethical text a *lieu de mémoire* in Pierre Nora's terms, where architecture stands as testimony to what societies choose to remember. To engage with the built environment, therefore, is to participate in the politics of remembering and forgetting. The responsibility of future urban planning lies not merely in sustaining infrastructures but in nurturing mnemonic landscapes that safeguard any city's historical memory.

To ensure such a future, the book proposes the systematic incorporation of Heritage Impact Assessments (HIA), community-based participatory models, and affective mapping into planning frameworks. These methods enable an inclusive negotiation between material heritage and lived memory, allowing urban policy to evolve from preservation as display to preservation as dialogue. Such interventions resist the homogenizing forces of global modernity by rooting spatial transformation into localized emotional geographies.

Layered Modernities: Memory as Structure in Contemporary Urbanism

Across the diverse urban case studies examined in this book from the adaptive restoration of Istanbul's Ottoman quarters to the revitalization of Mumbai's colonial arteries, and from the mnemonic landscapes of Hiroshima to the hydrological revivals of Jodhpur a discernible pattern emerges. A closer analysis can reveal that urban planning in the discussed instances in the earlier chapter resists the ideology of tabula rasa modernism. Rather than perceiving the city as a blank slate to be overwritten by the logic of modern efficiency, these projects reimagined the urban fabric as a palimpsest where traces of the past are not obstacles to progress but foundational elements of identity, continuity, and emotional resonance.

This refusal of erasure marks a critical departure from the modernist doctrines of the early twentieth century, epitomized by Le Corbusier's vision of a "machine for living" and by the sweeping urban renewal schemes that characterized postwar reconstruction. Such models, grounded in rationalist and functionalist principles, often sought to replace the misconstruction/destruction of historical cities with the orderliness of zoning, geometry, and uniformity. In doing so, they severed the visceral link between people and place reducing cities to abstract diagrams of circulation and production. Against this legacy, the urban projects discussed here embody what might be termed a mnemonic urbanism, where the past is not an inert residue but an active architectural material.

1. The Ethics of Refusal: From Erasure to Integration

The decision to layer rather than demolish reveals an ethical dimension in urban design , a recognition that memory constitutes a civic resource. To erase is to commit what Andreas Huyssen describes as "the violence of forgetting," an amnesia that alienates communities from their own spatial histories. The alternative, visible in Istanbul's adaptive reuse projects or Bhubaneswar's heritage corridors, lies in integration: embedding the memory of previous epochs within the infrastructural present. This process involves not merely the restoration of facades but the reactivation of symbolic, social, and sensory geographies allowing architecture to operate as an archive of lived experience.

Here, Henri Lefebvre's conceptual triad of space ; *conceived, perceived, and lived* proves indispensable. In these urban contexts, the conceived space of planners engages in a dialogue with the lived space of citizens. The result is a negotiated spatiality where top-down design accommodates bottom-up memory practices. Memory thus becomes a structural principle not decorative, but constitutive of urban structure.

2. The City as a *Textural* Layering:

The metaphor of the textural offers the most accurate conceptual language to describe these urban transformations. As Andreas Schönle observes, the palimpsest "translates the temporality of historical experience into spatial texture," allowing the city to manifest time in its very materiality. Istanbul, for instance, embodies this aesthetic of layering with remarkable clarity. Byzantine cisterns coexist beneath Ottoman mosques and modern glass towers, producing an architectural narrative of sedimented time. Rather than homogenizing the city's visual grammar, such coexistence affirms multiplicity as a mode of truth. Memory here is not merely preserved it is performed through architecture.

Similarly, Mumbai's Dadabhai Naoroji Road demonstrates how colonial memory can be negotiated rather than repudiated. Through the integration of restored facades, heritage lighting, and pedestrian-oriented design, the project resists both nostalgic paralysis and destructive modernization. It transforms the street into a living archive, where everyday movement and historical consciousness coalesce. In this sense, memory does not exist as static commemoration but as a dynamic spatial rhythm constantly renewed through human inhabitation.

3. Material Continuity and the Re-enchantment of Space

In refusing tabula rasa modernism, these urban interventions also generate what Tim Ingold calls the *re-enchantment of space* a reconnection between material form and affective experience. Materials such as stone, wood, and water are reintroduced not merely for their aesthetic or ecological value but for their mnemonic resonance. The Birkha Bawari Stepwell in Jodhpur, for example, reactivates the hydrological logic of premodern Rajasthan through sustainable design, transforming an ancient water system into a contemporary ecological landmark. The physical material earth, sandstone, and water—becomes an index of historical consciousness, reminding the present of the ingenuity embedded in its past.

In contrast to the disembodied modernist grid, such architecture restores tactility to urban life. Surfaces weather, textures retain traces, and spaces evoke ancestral rhythms. This sensory materiality is central to Maurice Halbwachs's understanding of collective memory, which insists that remembrance is sustained not by abstract ideas but by spatial frameworks that embody continuity. When the city retains its older materials and forms, it preserves not only physical structures but also the mnemonic scaffolding upon which social identity rests.

4. The Politics of Continuity

To layer rather than erase also signifies a political stance a refusal of the homogenizing narratives of nationalism and global capitalism that often demand aesthetic conformity. In the global South, especially, where postcolonial urbanism has oscillated between imitation of the West and recovery of indigenous traditions, memory-sensitive design functions as a politics of continuity. It acknowledges historical ruptures while rejecting the false dichotomy between tradition and modernity.

In Seoul's Seoullo 7017, the transformation of an obsolete overpass into a public walkway does not conceal the infrastructure's industrial past; it re-signifies it. Concrete, steel, and vegetation coexist as testimony to a city's evolving identity. Here, memory is ecological and political an act of reclaiming the urban surface for civic participation and historical consciousness. This layered approach also critiques the neoliberal aesthetic of erasure that underpins gentrification, reminding us that memory cannot be commodified without consequence.

5. Memory as Urban Method

Ultimately, these urban experiments illustrate how memory can evolve from a subject of cultural discourse to a method of design. Memory becomes a planning tool, shaping zoning policies, design codes, and heritage frameworks. Through mechanisms such as Heritage Impact Assessments (HIA), participatory mapping, and community consultations, planners integrate intangible heritage—the stories, rituals, and emotional geographies that animate built space into the design process. This epistemological shift redefines urban planning not as a science of control but as an art of remembrance.

The implication is profound: to build with memory is to build ethically. As Aldo Rossi contends, "the city itself is the collective memory of its people." In this sense, every act of design becomes an intervention in the temporal continuum of the city a negotiation between what must be retained and what can be transformed. Memory is no longer relegated to monuments; it is distributed across the city's surfaces, infrastructures, and atmospheres, making remembrance a structural condition of urban modernity.

Conclusion: The Architecture of Remembering

The pattern across all these cases thus reveals a paradigm shift from modernist erasure to mnemonic integration. By rejecting the blank-slate mentality, planners and architects reclaim the temporal depth of the city. The layering of past and present produces an architecture of remembering one that honors multiplicity, sustains continuity, and enables the coexistence of histories within the same spatial frame.

Such a model of urbanism anticipates a future where development does not annihilate memory but grows through it where cities evolve as living archives, composed not of linear progressions but of intricate temporal folds. The refusal of tabula rasa modernism, then, is not merely aesthetic; it is ontological and ethical. It redefines what it means to inhabit, design, and remember within the ever-changing text of the city. This book aspires to extend the frontiers of both literary and spatial inquiry by foregrounding memory as a critical epistemology for urban understanding. Its findings not only enrich interdisciplinary scholarship at the intersection of literature, architecture, and cultural geography but also gesture and suggestion toward a more humane model of urban planning one that resists the logic of erasure. By emphasizing the mnemonic and affective value embedded in existing architectures, it advocates for developmental practices ensuring that the evolving city retains the living testimonies of its past within the texture of its future form.

Works Cited
- Halbwachs, Maurice. *On Collective Memory*. Translated and edited by Lewis A. Coser, University of Chicago Press, 1992.
- Lefebvre, Henri. *The Production of Space*. Translated by Donald Nicholson-Smith, Blackwell, 1991.
- Le Corbusier. *Towards a New Architecture*. Translated by Frederick Etchells, Dover Publications, 1986.
- Le Corbusier. *The City of To-Morrow and Its Planning*. Translated by Frederick Etchells, Dover Publications, 1987.
- Rossi, Aldo. *The Architecture of the City*. Translated by Diane Ghirardo and Joan Ockman, MIT Press, 1982

References
- Abdulfatah, Mohammed, and Babasaheb Ambedkar. "A History of Two Cities: The Literature of Cairo and Istanbul." *ResearchGate*, vol. 7, no. 1, June 2022, pp. 198–203.
- Ahmed, S., and N. Ahmad. "Architectural Heritage and Cultural Identity: The Case of Hagia Sophia." *Journal of Cultural Heritage Studies*, 2022.

- Appadurai, Arjun. *Modernity at Large: Cultural Dimensions of Globalization.* University of Minnesota Press, 1996.
- Assmann, Aleida. *Cultural Memory and Western Civilization: Functions, Media, Archives.* Cambridge University Press, 2011.
- Assmann, Aleida, and Jan Assmann. *Cultural Memory and Early Civilization: Writing, Remembrance, and Political Imagination.* Cambridge University Press, 2011.
- Azoulay, Ariella Aïsha. *Potential History: Unlearning Imperialism.* Verso, 2019.
- Bachelard, Gaston. *The Poetics of Space.* Translated by Maria Jolas, Beacon Press, 1994.
- Bayraktaroglu, S., and D. Öktem Erkartal. "Urban Memory and the Architecture of Continuity in Istanbul." *Journal of Urban History and Heritage*, vol. 8, no. 2, 2020, pp. 31–34.
- Bozdoğan, Sibel. *Modernism and Nation Building: Turkish Architectural Culture in the Early Republic.* University of Washington Press, 2001.
- Butalia, Urvashi. *The Other Side of Silence: Voices from the Partition of India.* Penguin Books, 1998.
- Çelik, Zeynep. *The Remaking of Istanbul: Portrait of an Ottoman City in the Nineteenth Century.* University of California Press, 2004.
- Cormack, Robin. *Byzantine Art.* Oxford University Press, 2000.
- Das, Debojyoti. "Pilgrimage, Heritage, and Displacement: Politics of Temple Corridors in Puri." *Economic and Political Weekly*, vol. 57, no. 43, 2022, pp. 52–60.

- de Certeau, Michel. *The Practice of Everyday Life.* University of California Press, 1984.
- Dovey, Kim. *Becoming Places: Urbanism / Architecture / Identity / Power.* Routledge, 2010.
- Foucault, Michel. "Of Other Spaces." *Diacritics,* vol. 16, no. 1, 1986, pp. 22–27.
- Freely, John. *Istanbul: The Imperial City.* Penguin Books, 1998.
- Graham, Stephen, and Simon Marvin. *Splintering Urbanism: Networked Infrastructures, Technological Mobilities, and the Urban Condition.* Routledge, 2001.
- Halbwachs, Maurice. *On Collective Memory.* Edited and translated by Lewis A. Coser, University of Chicago Press, 1992.
- Harvey, David. *The Condition of Postmodernity: An Enquiry into the Origins of Cultural Change.* Blackwell, 1989.
- Hirsch, Marianne. *The Generation of Postmemory: Writing and Visual Culture after the Holocaust.* Columbia University Press, 2012.
- Huyssen, Andreas. *Present Pasts: Urban Palimpsests and the Politics of Memory.* Stanford University Press, 2003.
- Kalyoncu, Derya. "Spatial Narratives and Memory in Contemporary Istanbul." *Journal of Urban Cultural Studies,* vol. 7, no. 2, 2021, pp. 115–128.
- Kaya, Ayşe. "Continuity and Transformation in Istanbul's Urban Heritage." *Middle Eastern Architectural Review,* 2020.
- Kıvrak, Pelin. "Urban Imaginaries and the Politics of Memory in Contemporary Istanbul." *Journal of Cultural*

Memory Studies, vol. 4, no. 2, 2020, pp. 33–49.
- Lefebvre, Henri. *The Production of Space.* Translated by Donald Nicholson-Smith, Blackwell, 1991.
- Macdonald, Sharon. *Memorylands: Heritage and Identity in Europe Today.* Routledge, 2013.
- Massey, Doreen. *For Space.* Sage Publications, 2005.
- Nandy, Ashis. *An Ambiguous Journey to the City: The Village and Other Odd Ruins of the Self in the Indian Imagination.* Oxford University Press, 2001.
- Necipoğlu, Gülru. *The Age of Sinan: Architectural Culture in the Ottoman Empire.* Reaktion Books, 2005.
- Nora, Pierre. "Between Memory and History: Les Lieux de Mémoire." *Representations*, no. 26, 1989, pp. 7–24.
- Ousterhout, Robert. *Master Builders of Byzantium.* University of Pennsylvania Museum of Archaeology and Anthropology, 1999.
- Pamuk, Orhan. *Istanbul: Memories and the City.* Translated by Maureen Freely, Knopf, 2005.
- Pamuk, Orhan. *Istanbul: Memories and the City.* Translated by Maureen Freely, Alfred A. Knopf, 2005.
- Pamuk, Orhan. *The Museum of Innocence.* Translated by Maureen Freely, Alfred A. Knopf, 2009.
- Parui, Avishek. *Culture and the Literary: Matter, Metaphor, Memory.* Rowman & Littlefield, 2022.
- Parui, Avishek. *Memory, Identity and the Colonial Encounter in India: Essays in Criticism.* Routledge, 2022.
- Parui, Avishek. "Memory, Media and the Digital Self." *Memory Studies*, vol. 15, no. 3, 2022, pp. 1–15.
- Parui, Avishek, and Merin Simi Raj. "The Postdigital Postcolonial: A Study of the Anglo-Indian Community

through the Augmented Reality App MemoryBytes." *ResearchGate*, 2023.
- Ricoeur, Paul. *Memory, History, Forgetting.* University of Chicago Press, 2004.
- Rossi, Aldo. *The Architecture of the City.* Translated by Diane Ghirardo and Joan Ockman, MIT Press, 1982.
- Şahin, O. Erdal. "The Construction of Hagia Sophia as an Imperial Space and the Process of Change." *Balkan and Near Eastern Journal of Social Sciences*, vol. 5, no. 3, 2019–2020.
- Sargın, Güven Arif. "Displaced Memories, or the Architecture of Forgetting and Remembrance." *Environment and Planning D: Society and Space*, vol. 22, no. 5, 2004, pp. 659–680.
- Till, Karen E. *The New Berlin: Memory, Politics, Place.* University of Minnesota Press, 2005.
- Tuan, Yi-Fu. *Space and Place: The Perspective of Experience.* University of Minnesota Press, 1977.
- UNESCO. "Hiroshima Peace Memorial (Genbaku Dome)." *UNESCO World Heritage Centre*, 1996, whc.unesco.org/en/list/775.
- Volait, Mercedes, and Nazan Avcıoğlu. *Architectural Crossings: Byzantium and the Ottoman World.* Routledge, 2019.
- Young, James E. *The Texture of Memory: Holocaust Memorials and Meaning.* Yale University Press, 1993.

Black Eagle Books

www.blackeaglebooks.org
info@blackeaglebooks.org

Black Eagle Books, an independent publisher, was founded as a nonprofit organization in April, 2019. It is our mission to connect and engage the Indian diaspora and the world at large with the best of works of world literature published on a collaborative platform, with special emphasis on foregrounding Contemporary Classics and New Writing.

www.ingramcontent.com/pod-product-compliance
Lightning Source LLC
Chambersburg PA
CBHW060606080526
44585CB00013B/706